Disney



# FASCINATING FACTS

First published in the UK in 2024 by Studio Press,
an imprint of Bonnier Books UK,
4th Floor, Victoria House, Bloomsbury Square, London WC1B 4DA
Owned by Bonnier Books,
Sveavägen 56, Stockholm, Sweden

bonnierbooks.co.uk



1 3 5 7 9 10 8 6 4 2


ISBN 978-1-80078-821-3

Written by Craig Jelley
Edited by Frankie Jones
Cover designed by Maddox Philpot
Interiors designed by Alessandro Susin
Production by Giulia Caparrelli

FSC
www.fsc.org
MIX
Paper | Supporting responsible forestry
FSC® C018072

A CIP catalogue record for this book is available from the British Library
Printed and bound in Great Britain by Clays Ltd, Elcograf S.p.A.

Disney

# FASCINATING FACTS

**OVER 1,000 REAL-WORLD FACTS FOR CURIOUS MINDS**

STUDIO PRESS

**WELCOME TO DISNEY FASCINATING FACTS, A BUMPER BOOK OF THE MOST INCREDIBLE, ASTOUNDING AND, OFTEN, DOWNRIGHT UNUSUAL ITEMS OF INFORMATION THAT YOU'LL EVER LAY YOUR EYES ON.**

It doesn't matter whether you're looking to fill your brain with bundles of trivia, pick up some amazing info to wow your friends with or just discover more about the fascinating world we live in, there's sure to be something for you among over 1,000 incredible facts!

Flick through these pages of tantalising trivia and you'll discover sections dedicated to everything from insects and biology to planets and Ancient Greece. With so many facts spanning so many different subjects, you're bound to find something that piques your curiosity, no matter what mood you're in.

Have you ever wondered what the smell of freshly cut grass is? If you dive into the Nature section, you'll uncover the unexpected answer. Have you heard the one about the book that predicted an international disaster? No, it's not a joke, but a spooky coincidence that can be found in the Arts chapter. Maybe you've wondered whether or not Blackbeard was a real pirate and if so, who was he? The answers ye seek are buried in the pages devoted to History.

These tidbits are just a few tasters of the trivia you will traverse on your journey through this fact-packed book, so if you're sufficiently intrigued, what are you waiting for? Turn the page!

# NATURE

Whether you're looking at the creepy-crawlies beneath your feet, or the starry sky above you, you're surrounded by the amazing natural world. Read on to discover incredible trivia about everything from mosquitoes and polar bears to talking mushrooms and bright stars millions of kilometres away!

As well as being delicious, strawberries are one of the few fruits that grow their seeds on the outside – sometimes up to 200 of them. In fact, they're technically not called seeds, but something called an achene, which is an individual fruit that holds a seed.

The biggest flower in the world is the Rafflesia arnoldii. It can grow to over 1 metre wide. It doesn't have its own root system, so latches onto other plants to grow. Don't sniff this flower though – its smell has been likened to rotting meat.

Ferns are some of the oldest plants on Earth. They've been around since before the Mesozoic Era, which was when dinosaurs took their first steps on the planet, over 360 million years ago.

Pitcher plants have jug-shaped leaves and produce a nectar that entices insects and other small creatures inside. The leaves of the pitcher plant close once an animal falls in, and chemicals called enzymes digest the creature so the plant can use the nutrients.

No plant grows faster than bamboo. A Chinese bamboo variety called moso can grow almost 1 metre in a single day. It doesn't waste its energy growing any wider, so it can concentrate on shooting straight up.

Some animals only eat plants, but sometimes the plants bite back! The Venus fly trap has hinged leaves that look like a toothy mouth. If an insect touches the hairs inside the leaves, they snap shut so the insect can't escape. It can take the Venus fly trap up to five days to digest the trapped insect.

There are around 73,000 species of tree on Earth, and amazingly over 50 percent of them can only be found in a single country! If you want to see the most unique trees in one trip, Brazil, Colombia and Indonesia top the charts for most native trees.

Tulips were introduced to Europe in the 16th century from Turkey. In the 17th century, particularly in the Netherlands, the demand was so great that they were said to be more expensive than gold. However, the mania faded and left lots of people with a very expensive plant collection that they couldn't sell on.

Summer means giant sunflowers cropping up all over the place. But did you know that the 'flower' of a sunflower is pseudanthium, or flowerhead, and is actually made up of many small flowers?

The Wolffia family of plants, also known as duckweed or watermeal, grow on the top of water and include the smallest flowering plants. Wolffia can be grown from seed, but can also clone itself very quickly too. The fastest recorded clone took just under 30 hours to produce.

The oldest documented tree in the world is known as Methuselah, a Great Basin bristlecone pine that grows in the White Mountains of California, USA. It has lived for over 4,800 years.

The baobab tree, sometimes known as the 'tree of life', is found largely on the continents of Africa and Australia. They can be massive in height and circumference, with some species reaching up to 25 metres tall and others 25 metres around.

The tallest tree in the world is a coastal redwood in California, known as Hyperion. Coastal redwoods can grow super tall, but Hyperion is the biggest of them all, measuring just over 116 metres. Experts think it's somewhere between 600 and 800 years old.

Some fungi communicate via a system of underground threads called mycelium, which can connect them across several kilometres. If one of the fungi is being eaten, it will send a signal through the mycelium to warn others and allow them to disperse a repellent chemical.

Everybody loves the smell of freshly cut grass, but the smell is actually a distress call that the grass is giving off. When cut, the grass releases pheromones that some scientists believe is a call of help against the attack.

The jaboticaba tree, also known as the Brazilian grape tree, doesn't have fruit dangling from branches like apples and lemons. Instead, the fruit grows directly from the trunk of the tree, so it looks like it's covered in big juicy boils.

We all know that trees need sunlight and water to survive, but exactly how much water do they need? Some oak trees can drink up to 450 litres of water a day, but that's nothing compared to the giant sequoia, which will guzzle up to four times that.

You can tell the age of most trees when they're chopped down by counting the number of rings the trunk has, but it can also show how well the tree has grown each year. The ring will be thicker if it has had an abundance of resources, or thinner when there haven't been as many.

If you're lost in the woods, you may be able to use trees and moss to navigate your way home. In the northern hemisphere, the sun shines more from the south, so damp- and dark-loving moss will form on the north side of tree bark. If you're in the southern hemisphere, the opposite is true, but either will give you a direction to work with.

Clusters of bananas are known as 'hands' when they grow on trees. You can probably see why – because they look like bunches of yellow fingers.

There's a place called the Alnwick Garden in the United Kingdom that has a poison garden, which is filled exclusively with over a hundred poisonous plants. It's so dangerous that you're only allowed to enter it with a tour guide.

Many plants protect themselves with deadly toxins, but the oleander is one of the most poisonous to humans. If eaten, the leaves of an oleander plant can cause problems with the heart, nerves and stomach, and can even be deadly.

Giving a bouquet of flowers is a lovely gesture, but they end up dying quite quickly, even when in water. Tulips actually grow by up to 2.5 centimetres a day after they've been chopped, though they will die eventually.

The United Kingdom has 'ancient woodlands', which are classified as forests that have had trees since the year 1600. One of the largest of these is Sherwood Forest, home of the fabled Robin Hood, where over a thousand trees are thought to be over a thousand years old.

The rarest orchid in the world is the critically endangered ghost orchid. It's native to Florida, the Bahamas and Cuba, has a pale white flower and absolutely no leaves. It gets all the energy it needs from the trees it wraps around. Only 2,000 ghost orchids are thought to exist.

There's a type of grass native to Africa that's known as elephant grass, and it can grow over four metres tall. It's so called because, at that height, it's tall enough to hide an elephant! However, elephants also eat the grass, ruining all their best hiding spots.

Scientists in Russia were able to grow a plant from seeds they found in a 32,000-year-old squirrel burrow. The seeds were buried about 38 metres below the tundras of the Siberia region and grew into relatives of the modern narrow-leafed campion.

Some prehistoric fossils aren't housed in rock, but rather a substance called amber. This translucent orange substance is fossilised tree resin, which is a sticky sap that most trees make. Fossilised amber often contains prehistoric insects, such as mosquitoes and damselflies.

Most flowers hate the winter months, preferring to bloom in sunnier seasons, but the skunk cabbage has a clever trick. Unlike other flowers, it can produce heat itself, which melts away the snow and frost that threaten it.

The *Welwitschia mirabilis* plant is found in the northern Namib Desert, in southern Africa. It will only ever grow two leaves in its lifetime, but they can grow up to 6 metres long. However, the leaves split over time into multiple segments, making the plant appear to have more leaves.

A rose by any other name... could be a peach! The beautiful family of roses also counts a few unusual inclusions among its members. Strawberry, peach, quince, pear, apple and apricot plants are all from the same family as the rose.

Most plant roots stretch a few centimetres into the ground to collect sustenance. But there's a wild fig tree in South Africa that has roots sinking over 120 metres deep. They were discovered when they poked through an underground spot called Echo Cave.

Before trees shot up on Earth, the largest plant was an ancient fungus called a prototaxite. It's believed that this fungus could grow up to 8 metres tall and almost 1 metre wide, but didn't have caps like mushrooms we see today!

The oldest species of tree in the world is the ginkgo, sometimes known as ginkgo biloba. Fossils of the tree have been dated back almost 200 million years, which means it outlasted the dinosaurs.

As the majority of the Earth's oxygen comes from the sea, you'd expect there to be lots of plant life, but only around 14 percent of plant life exists underwater. This includes algae, kelp, plankton, seagrass and sargassum.

Oak trees are struck by lightning more than any other tree. Some believe it's because they're often the tallest trees around, while others point to a water-filled centre and deep roots that make them good conductors of electricity. Either way, steer clear of oaks in a storm!

About 70 percent of our planet's surface is ocean, but over 80 percent of it is unmapped. The ocean is home to more than 240,000 species, but scientists estimate a figure anywhere between 700,000 and 1.6 million!

The Challenger Deep, found in the Mariana Trench in the Pacific Ocean, is the deepest point in the world's ocean. Only 22 people have ever explored it, down to a depth of around 11,000 metres below sea level. No one has ever even reached the bottom.

The sea off the coast of North Carolina, in the United States, is nicknamed the 'Graveyard of the Atlantic' because so many ships have sunk there. The ocean floor there is estimated to be littered with the wreckage of more than 2,000 ships.

The ocean is a big place. Some parts of the ocean are warm. Some parts are cold. Ocean floors have mountains and valleys and even forests made of kelp. Different parts of the ocean are home to many different creatures.

The water in a maelstrom – a powerful whirlpool in a sea or ocean – swirls into a central vortex, like bathwater down a drain. The world's strongest maelstrom is in the channel of Saltstraumen, in Norway, where whirlpools can reach up to 10 metres across and speeds of up to 40 km/h.

There is only one global ocean, but in world maps it is usually divided into five named oceans: the Pacific, the Atlantic, the Indian, the Arctic and the Southern. Smaller areas of water where the land meets the water are often called seas, such as the Adriatic Sea, which is the water between Italy to the west and primarily Croatia and Albania to the east.

The Bermuda Triangle, made up of points in Bermuda, Puerto Rico and Florida, is part of the Atlantic Ocean where many aircraft and ships have disappeared without a trace. Experts say there is no evidence that vessels go missing in the Bermuda Triangle more often than in other places and that there is nothing mysterious about this region...

Colourful coral reefs, like the one Nemo and Marlin call home in *Finding Nemo*, grow best in shallow, sunlit ocean waters and are always teeming with plant and animal life.

Kelp is one of the fastest-growing life forms on the planet and can increase its size by up to 45 centimetres in a single day. Kelp forests often grow in rough and choppy water, which keeps the fresh nutrients flowing to the kelp.

The Great Barrier Reef, found off the coast of Australia, is the largest coral reef in the world. At more than 2,000 kilometres long, it is the biggest living structure on Earth – so big that you can see it from space! It's home to sea turtles, stingrays, seahorses, and hundreds of other animals.

Algae is one of the oldest living things on the planet and often covers coral reefs. It gets its energy from the sun, which it turns into oxygen. In fact, up to 70 percent of the oxygen in Earth's atmosphere is made by algae. More importantly, blue tangs like Dory from *Finding Nemo* eat algae and stop it from damaging the coral.

The water in the Dead Sea, found between Israel and Jordan, is ten times saltier than the oceans of the world, which makes it much more dense than normal water. If you swim in it, the water's density will automatically make you float.

There are two ice sheets – massive masses of ice – left over from Earth's last ice age. One of them, the Antarctic Ice Sheet, is 14 million square kilometres, which is the size of the USA and Mexico combined.

The sea has canyons too! The Grand Canyon in the USA is over 1,800 metres deep at its deepest point, but underwater crevasses like the Zhemchug Canyon in the Bering Sea are even deeper, reaching a depth of 2,600 metres.

In 1997, scientists recorded an unusual sound, which they called 'the bloop', from a distance of over 3,200 kilometres away. It took them eight years to discover that it was an icequake – the sound of an iceberg cracking away from a glacier.

A tsunami is a series of giant waves that can catastrophically hit land, causing millions of pounds worth of damage, as well as injury and death. They're caused by seismic activity like earthquakes and can reach speeds of up to 800 km/h.

We might not ever see them, but the ocean produces waves over 200 metres tall. These 'internal waves' travel thousands of kilometres at a time, but they're all underwater. If they were on the surface, they'd cause wreckages on every coast.

The longest mountain range isn't the Andes, which is only the longest mountain range on land, but the underwater Mid-Ocean Ridge. It meanders around most of the oceans in the world and is over 64,000 kilometres long – just over seven times longer than the Andes!

The furthest-away point from land in the ocean is found in the Pacific Ocean, around 2,700 kilometres from the nearest land. It's called Point Nemo, but not after everyone's favourite clownfish! It's actually named after Captain Nemo in the novel *Twenty Thousand Leagues Under the Sea* by Jules Verne.

If all of the ice in the sea – glaciers, ice sheets and icebergs – melted, scientists believe the ocean would rise globally about 70 metres. That's enough to cover the majority of the world's land and even consume most of the Statue of Liberty.

The Pacific Ocean is the world's largest named ocean, and covers about 30 percent of the planet's surface. It is bordered by more than 50 different countries and is home to over 25,000 different islands.

In some parts of the ocean, the water can become denser thanks to something called hydrogen sulphide. The denser water can pool together to form underwater rivers, lakes and waterfalls.

The tallest underwater waterfall is called the Denmark Strait cataract, which has a descent of 3,200 metres. It's created by cold water falling over a cliff near dense areas of water and is more than three times the height of the biggest land-based waterfall, Angel Falls in Venezuela.

Have you ever wondered why water is clear, but the ocean is blue? The water in the ocean filters out colours from the light spectrum, like red, leaving behind just the blue hues. Blue light also goes much further than other lights, which is why it gets bluer as you go deeper... and it gets darker too!

The oceans are the biggest habitat in the world and over 98 percent of life calls the ocean home. That's incredible when you think of how many humans, animals and plants there are on the land around you!

There's enough gold in the ocean to give everybody on Earth 4 kilograms of the stuff! Unfortunately, the gold exists as tiny particles dissolved in the ocean itself, or in mineral veins that are too difficult to mine.

More than 80 percent of the ocean has never been mapped or visited by people. Because it's so dark after a certain depth and the pressure is too great when the water is deep, it makes it very hard to venture into new parts of the ocean. Who knows what else is lurking deep below the surface?

There is a series of currents in the ocean that can take a drop of water around every inch of the ocean. It's known as the global ocean conveyor belt and it changes direction based on the temperatures and salt content of the water. The journey of that drop of water, though, would take over one thousand years!

The ocean is estimated to be home to over one million volcanoes. Thankfully, most of them aren't active. However, underwater volcanic activity makes up over 80 percent of all volcano eruptions on the planet.

There are over 804,000 kilometres worth of network cables lying on the ocean floor, which connect the high-speed internet across continents. These cables carry over 95 percent of global communications. Think about that the next time you send an email!

The pressure – the force that an object has to withstand – in the deepest waters is immense. In the Challenger Deep, the deepest known part of the ocean, the pressure is the equivalent of one hundred elephants standing on the head of a nail.

The Mariana Trench is the world's least visited place that we know about due to its extreme depth. Only ten more people have been to the Mariana Trench than the moon, despite needing a rocket to get to Earth's satellite.

If the pressure at extreme depths wasn't enough to worry about, there are also parts of the ocean called hydrothermal vents that are extremely hot too. Temperatures around these areas can reach up to 400°C!

Coral has a symbiotic relationship with the algae that lives on it. Algae lives in the tissue of coral and the coral in turn uses the algae for sustenance, which gives it colour. If the ocean's conditions turn for the worse, the algae departs, which leaves the coral bleached.

So many ships have sunk in the oceans across history, that some people believe that Earth's oceans have more artefacts in it than all of the museums in the world combined! However, it's much harder to visit these underwater 'museums'...

A shipment of rubber ducks was accidentally dropped into the Pacific Ocean in 1992, but oceanographers turned it into an opportunity. They asked people all over the world to get in touch when a rubber duck washed ashore so they could better understand the currents in the Pacific.

Hydrothermal vents, places where boiling, mineral-rich fluid squirts out of the sea floor – are teeming with creatures that don't need sunlight to survive, such as the yeti crab. They change chemicals into energy without the help of sunlight.

Wild horses were first domesticated over 6,000 years ago, and they have been part of countless expeditions since then. Between 1994 and 2014, an adventurer named Günter Wamser rode on horseback from the southernmost tip of South America to Alaska – a distance of more than 25,000 km.

The Xoloitzcuintli (shoh-loh-its-KWINT-lee) is a mostly hairless breed of dog, just like Dante from *Coco*! Xolo dogs have been present in Mexico for thousands of years. They were sacred guides and companions of the Aztecs in daily life.

Whale sharks such as Destiny from *Finding Dory* live in the warmer oceans of the world and can dive thousands of feet under the water. They are filter feeders – they swim with their mouths open, sucking in water filled with plankton, tiny fish and krill. Then they filter the water through their gills and eat whatever is left.

Some indigenous Mexicans revered jaguars and believed they had godlike abilities of power and courage, but they're now in danger of becoming extinct due to habitat loss and illegal hunting. The Mexican government and protection groups preserve land where the cats can live in peace.

Blue tangs like Dory from *Finding Nemo* are saltwater fish that live in warm coral reefs and rocky waters close to shore. They're from a family of fish called surgeonfish, so called because they all have at least one sharp blade next to their tail, which they use to protect themselves when threatened.

Dory's friend Bailey from *Finding Dory* is a beluga whale, which is a type of mammal and not a fish. Toothed whales like the beluga use sound to find and measure the shapes of things, which is called echolocation. They make a clicking sound that bounces off objects, then listen for the echo to map out where they are.

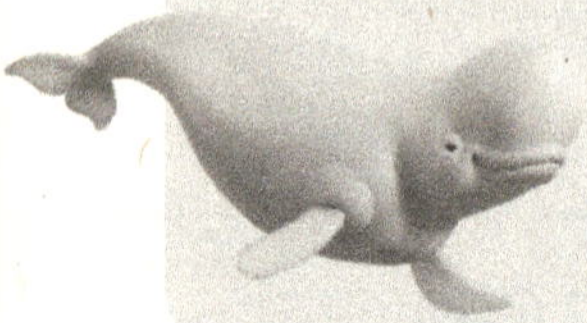

Under their skin, whales are covered from head to toe in blubber, which is a thick layer of fat that keeps warm-blooded whales at a comfortable temperature in the cold ocean. Fish don't need blubber because they're cold-blooded – it's already the same temperature as the water around them.

Clownfish like Nemo from *Finding Nemo* live in the tentacles of sea anemones on coral reefs. Sea anemones are covered in poisonous tentacles, but clownfish are covered in a slime that protects them from being affected, keeping them safe from predators near the anemone.

Mr Ray from *Finding Nemo* is a spotted eagle ray. Rays swim by moving their whole bodies like a wave and some also flap their side pectoral fins like wings. One kind of ray, the roughtail stingray, can move really fast – up to 48 km/h.

The blue whale is the largest animal on the planet. They can be 30 metres long and weigh up to 199 tonnes. Blue whales have two blowholes and no teeth. They live all over the world. Unlike beluga whales and dolphins, they usually live alone.

California sea lions like Fluke and Rudder from *Finding Dory* normally cruise along at 17 km/h, but can swim in bursts of up to 40 km/h. That's pretty fast for an animal that can weigh 272 kilograms. They can also dive almost 300 metres under the water, holding their breath the whole time.

There's a mysterious whale that scientists have been tracking for over 30 years, that sings at a frequency unlike any other whale. The whale, known as 52 Blue, or just 52, calls out at a frequency of 52 hertz, which is higher than the closest species, the blue and fin whales, and sounds very odd to any whale that can hear it.

Sea anemone may be pretty... but they're also dangerous. They spend their whole lives attached to something hard, waving their tentacles around and waiting for a fish to swim too close. When it does, the sea anemone's tentacle shoots out a poison dart, stunning the fish, and then pulls the fish into its mouth.

Sea stars, or starfish, live in every type of ocean habitat including tidal pools, rocky shores, sea grass, kelp beds and coral reefs. They belong to a family of spiny-skinned animals, or echinoderms, which also includes sea cucumbers, sea urchins and sand dollars. Starfish move very slowly, holding on with many tiny suction-cupped tube feet. They can regrow an arm if they lose one.

The darkest depths of the ocean are home to a very interesting animal called the anglerfish. This funny-looking fish dangles a small light above its head to attract curious fish towards it. When they get close, it swallows them up!

Octopuses have tiny cells under their skin that can change colour so they can match their surroundings. Octopuses are so good at this that they can even make their skin appear bumpy or spiky to look more like the material they're hiding against.

There are over 300 kinds of octopuses – just like Hank from *Finding Dory* – in the world's oceans. They all have eight tentacles... and three hearts! They swim by taking water in through their heads and squirting it out behind them. But those tentacles aren't just for show – octopuses use them to crawl across the ocean floor.

Most fish have some sort of skeleton, but a shark doesn't have any bones at all. Its whole skeleton is made of cartilage. This means sharks are very flexible and can twist themselves quickly to catch speedy prey.

Flying squirrels have flaps of skin that stretch from their front to rear paws. A flying squirrel can jump from a tall tree, then spread its legs wide to create air resistance as it falls. This force slows the squirrel down so that it glides instead of falling.

Earth's fastest land animal is the cheetah. It can run at bursts of 114 km/h, while the speediest creature in the sea is the sailfish. This super swimmer can reach speeds of 110 km/h.

Some animals can walk on water! Lizards called basilisks can run for about 4.6 metres before sinking underwater. Birds called western grebes also run on water during take-off. A combination of speed, webbed feet, and surface tension makes this feat possible.

An animal called the pistol shrimp has a built-in blaster. This little critter has one huge claw that it can snap with incredible force. The snap makes a blast of sound and heat strong enough to stun other animals. Syndrome from *The Incredibles* would be proud!

There are very few native land mammals in the Pacific Islands. In Fiji, the only native land mammals are bats. But what about Pua and Heihei from *Moana*? Pigs and chickens were brought to the Pacific Islands thousands of years ago.

Some types of flea can jump up to 200 times the length of their body! They have a powerful springy protein that they squeeze when their legs fold, ready to jump. When they stop squeezing it, the protein creates explosive energy that makes the legs spring forward powerfully.

Lots of animals live in the harsh tundras of Earth. These include owls, foxes, wolves and reindeer. Foxes and reindeer have thick fur that protects them from the cold. Arctic wolves have fur on their paws that give them a better grip on the icy ground. Some animals, like huskies, even help people get around! These dogs are very strong and can pull sleds for a long time.

As well as reaching speeds of up to 96 km/h, the hummingbird is known for another fast feat. The tiniest species can flap their wings at a rate of 80 beats a second, or 4,800 times in one minute. And that's not all – their hearts can beat 1,200 times per minute too.

You might think that flamingos are pink, but those feathers are actually dyed. They eat a diet of blue-green algae and brine shrimp that contains a dye called canthaxanthin, which gives their feathers their pink colour.

Many animals have natural armour. The pangolin, for instance, is covered with hard, overlapping scales, while crocodiles are covered with bony knobs. Crabs and many other creatures have exoskeletons – where they wear their skeletons on the outside to protect the soft organs inside.

What do you think the world's deadliest animal is? The surprising answer is the mosquito. This annoying insect kills over 700,000 people a year by spreading diseases, such as malaria and yellow fever, when they bite.

Females carry babies in all known species of the animal kingdom... except one: the seahorse. The male seahorse gets pregnant and carries the young. They can give birth to up to one thousand babies at a time.

Axolotls are amazing amphibians related to salamanders. They can regrow lost limbs and organs like their heart and parts of their brain. They also don't scar when healing these parts, which scientists think could help humans to master regeneration!

Humans use the manure from cows to fertilise crops and fields. It's very lucky we have a use for it, as a single cow can poo up to 15 times a day, creating over 13,000 kilograms of the stuff every year. Stinky!

The giraffe is the tallest land animal in the world and can reach up to 5.5 metres tall! Their super-long necks give them their height, but they can't bend them enough to reach the floor, which is why they eat leaves from trees.

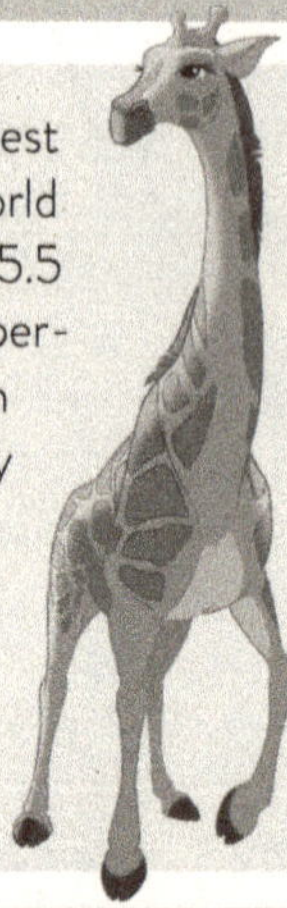

The peregrine falcon is the fastest animal in the world... but only when it's diving. When swooping down to catch prey, gravity helps to speed its descent and it has been recorded at speeds of 390 km/h.

The noisy rooster protects its ear from its morning cock-a-doodle by tilting its head back when it crows. Doing this blocks the ear canal of the rooster, so it doesn't suffer any damage from the sound it makes, which can reach up to 100 decibels.

Possibly the most impressive animal is almost invisible to the naked eye. The tardigrade, sometimes known as a water bear, measures just half a millimetre, can survive without food for up to 30 years and can withstand temperatures below −272°C!

A polar bear is white, right? Wrong! The skin of a polar bear is actually black, while its fur is mostly translucent – or see-through. Polar bears appear white because of the light reflecting off the snow and ice around them.

Japanese macaques – a type of monkey – sometimes live in the snowy areas of Japan's islands. They keep themselves warm by bathing in water heated by nearby volcanic activity and have been known to make and throw snowballs at each other!

Be wary of any suspicious koalas. Along with humans and primates, they're the only species in the world to have fingerprints. In fact, koala fingerprints are very hard to distinguish from human ones!

Cuckoos aren't the greatest parents. Instead of building their own nests, these birds lay their eggs in the nest of other bird species, who will take care of the chick as if it were its own. This means the mother cuckoo doesn't have to waste time sitting on an egg!

Chameleons change colour using pigments under their transparent skin. The brain sends a message to make certain pigments bigger or smaller so they can blend into their surroundings. They also use this to adapt to temperature, as they turn darker to absorb more heat, or lighter to cool down.

Scientists use GPS technology to track many wild animals, including sea turtles. Receivers are glued to the turtles' shells to collect location information wherever the turtles go. This information helps scientists understand the turtles' habits and needs, which helps in conservation efforts.

Some animals mark their territory by weeing or pooing, but the wombat takes this to another level. Because round poo can sometimes roll away from territory they're trying to mark, wombats have evolved to excrete cubes of poo!

The heaviest snake in the world is the green anaconda. The heaviest ever recorded was 227 kilograms and measured over a metre thick. It was over 8 metres long, but that isn't even the longest snake. One reticulated python was measured to be 10 metres long in the early 20th century!

Possums are the only marsupial found in North America and they have a clever defence mechanism against predators: they play dead. However, it's not entirely on purpose. The possum can get so scared that it stops in its tracks and falls over, sometimes for hours!

The bilby is a nocturnal marsupial found in Australia that's about the size of a rat and has long, pointy ears. It doesn't need to drink water because it gets all the liquid it needs from the food it eats.

The snake with the deadliest venom is the inland taipan, which can be found in Australia. Its bite delivers a mix of toxins that can paralyse muscles, prevent breathing and cause muscles and blood vessels to stop working.

Humans can only regrow their teeth once, but crocodiles can regrow theirs over and over throughout their lifetime. Some crocodiles can grow a full set of teeth 50 times during their life!

Climate change means that the world is getting warmer. The Earth experienced its eight hottest years in recorded history between 2015 and 2022, demonstrating the dangerous rise in global temperatures.

Internal combustion engines burn fuel which is not good for our air. More and more cars are being manufactured without internal combustion engines. Their engines use electricity for fuel, instead of petrol, which creates fewer emissions and is better for the environment. Even better for the environment is using public or active transport!

Barrow Island in Australia holds the record for the fastest wind speed. On 10 April 1996, Cyclone Olivia battered the island with a 408 km/h blast – the highest non-tornado wind speed ever recorded on Earth.

If you live in a city, you might have to deal with light pollution. Light pollution means that the lights on Earth are too bright, which blocks out the light of the stars. A full moon can also add to light pollution. The light from the full moon is so bright that it can make it hard to see many stars.

Some rubbish stays in our ecosystem for hundreds of years. Most plastics can take up to one thousand years to completely degrade, while glass takes four times as long to deteriorate! Fortunately, glass can be recycled completely and indefinitely. Only some plastics can be recycled, and they can only be recycled a certain number of times.

When cows parp, they release methane, which is one of the gases causing our climate to warm. Each cow can release around 90 kilograms of methane a year!

When trees are first turned into paper, the resultant sheets can be recycled up to six times before the fibres become too unstable to stick together. Recycling paper can stop humans needing to cut down as many trees.

More than 70 percent of the emissions of carbon dioxide – a harmful greenhouse gas – come from just a small collection of countries. China, the USA, Russia, Japan, India, Canada and the European Union are the largest emitters.

There are two massive man-made patches of rubbish floating in the ocean. The Great Pacific Garbage Patch is floating in the Pacific Ocean between the USA and Japan and consists of rubbish that isn't biodegradable – or won't deteriorate naturally – like plastic.

In 2016, Japanese scientists discovered bacteria, known as *Ideonella sakaiensis*, which has a unique diet. Rather than eating biological matter as most bacteria do, it digests a type of plastic! They believe these bacteria could help fight plastic pollution.

As a result of climate change, the sea levels around the world have risen by about 10 centimetres over the last 25 years. If this rate of rising levels continues, seas like the Mediterranean will rise another 1.2 metres by the year 2100, swallowing up coastal cities such as Venice.

Setting off in 2015 and landing in 2016, the airplane *Solar Impulse 2* flew around the world in 25 days powered by nothing but solar energy. It stored the required energy during a five-month span, and took off using the solar power, before gliding on huge wings to its next stop.

Microplastics are a type of pollutant made of plastic fragments that have broken down over time. They can cause harm to humans and to other creatures, particularly those that live in water, as they're now found in almost every sea and ocean on the planet.

There's a region of exceptionally depleted ozone in the stratosphere – which is a layer surrounding Earth that protects from the sun's harmful rays – over Antarctica, which appears every Spring. It was caused by man-made chemicals called CFCs, which were used in aerosols, but is on its way to healing thanks to CFCs being banned. Success!

If everyone in the world became vegetarian and didn't eat meat, the emissions from farming could decrease by 63 percent. If we stopped eating any animal products and became vegan, they could decrease by another 7 percent.

It's estimated that by the year 2050, there will be more plastic in the world's oceans than fish. And when you consider that trillions of fish are swimming around, you can imagine how much plastic is making its way to our waters.

Around 30 percent of carbon dioxide made by humans is absorbed into the ocean, which makes the water more acidic and negatively affects marine life, such as coral, as well as their habitats.

Energy from renewable sources, like solar and hydroelectric, now accounts for more of our global energy consumption than coal. In 2021, renewable sources generated 38 percent of the world's electricity, whereas coal only produced 36.5 percent.

The first effective solar cell, which is used to harness the power of the sun and turn it into a renewable energy source, was created in 1941 by Russell Ohl. But the process that makes it possible, called the photovoltaic effect, was first discovered in 1839.

Aluminium is the best material to use for food containers as you can recycle it limitlessly. Recycling an aluminium can saves 90 percent of the energy it would take to mine a new load from the Earth.

Solar energy can be stored in... salt! Sunlight is used to heat salt to over 130°C and turn it into a liquid. It's stored for up to a week and is then used to produce steam by heating water, just like fossil fuels do.

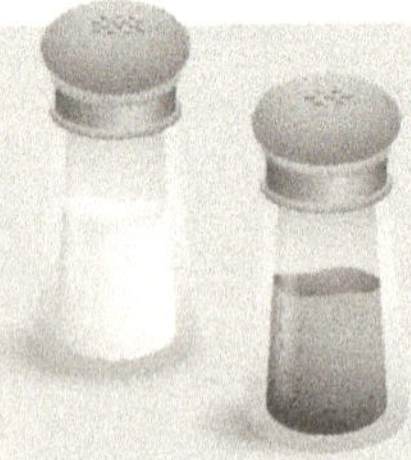

The tiny nation of Iceland was the first country in the world to produce almost all of its energy from renewable sources. It takes advantage of the geothermal properties of its land – the earth beneath Iceland is very hot – to achieve this.

Less than 1 percent of the Earth's water is drinkable – 97 percent is salt water in seas and oceans. The remaining fresh water (over 2 percent) is either part of glaciers, or too polluted to be fit for humans to drink.

As Earth spins on its axis, a star called Polaris – or the North Star – seems to sit still above the North Pole while all the other stars rotate around it. This makes Polaris easy to find from the Northern Hemisphere. You can look for the motionless star and use it to navigate.

If you're in the Southern Hemisphere, you can use a constellation called the Southern Cross to help you navigate. The long bar of the cross points to the South Celestial Pole. This is the point in the sky directly above the South Pole.

Do you know why day turns into night? It's because our planet is always spinning. Earth makes one full spin on its axis every 24 hours. The side facing the sun experiences day, while the side facing away from the sun is cast into night.

The earliest known drawn maps don't show Earth, they show the stars. One star map, drawn on the wall of a cave in France, dates from 14,500 BC. A star map drawn in another cave in Spain dates from 12,000 BC.

In the Southern Hemisphere, the aurora is called the Southern Lights or Aurora Australis. It can be seen from parts of New Zealand, Australia, South America and Antarctica. The farther you get from the Equator, the more likely you are to see auroras, which are collectively called the Polar Lights.

The aurora seen from the northernmost parts of Earth is called the Northern Lights, also known as the Aurora Borealis. It's a phenomenon created when electrons from the sun hit the gases in our atmosphere and make sparks. These sparks can be a flash of colour and if there are a lot of these crashes when the sky is dark and clear, we see the aurora.

We experience different seasons because Earth is tilted. The tilt of the Earth changes how high the sun gets in the sky – the higher the sun is, the warmer Earth gets. When the sun is highest, it's summer. When it's lowest, it's winter. In between, we have autumn and spring.

Giant groups of stars are called galaxies. Our sun is part of a spiral galaxy called the Milky Way, along with at least 100 billion other stars. It takes our sun more than 230 million years to orbit the centre of the galaxy. From Earth, what we can see of our galaxy looks like a milky band across the sky, which is where its name comes from.

A constellation is a group of stars that form a shape in the sky. Throughout history, people have used constellations to help them navigate. Have you heard of the Big Dipper? It is part of a constellation called Ursa Major, or 'Great Bear'. The two stars at the end of the dipper point directly at the North Star.

Our sun is the closest star to Earth and we make a full orbit around it once a year. The Sun is about 150 million kilometres away from us and 4.5 billion years old. At its centre, the Sun is around 15 million°C. Wow, that's hot!

Of the twenty brightest stars we can see with just our eyes, the most remote is called Deneb. It is part of the Cygnus constellation and is over 1,500 light-years away.

In many countries, the summer solstice is the first day of summer. It's the longest day of the year. The winter solstice is the shortest day of the year and marks the first day of winter in many places. When day and night are the same length, it's called an equinox. There are two of those each year – one in the autumn and one in the spring.

There are eight planets in our solar system. The closest planet to the Sun is Mercury, which travels around the Sun in only 88 days. The farthest planet is Neptune, which takes 165 years to orbit the Sun. Pluto is even further away but is a dwarf planet because it's so small!

Solar eclipses happen when the Moon gets between Earth and the Sun. There are two to five solar eclipses each year, with a total eclipse occurring once every 18 months. A total solar eclipse happens when the Sun, the Moon and Earth are in a straight line. If you're in the right place, the Sun and the sky will go dark during the day – but only for a few minutes.

A lunar eclipse happens when Earth gets in between the Sun and the Moon and casts its shadow on the Moon. We can still see the Moon during a total lunar eclipse because some light gets bent by Earth's atmosphere and hits the Moon, which makes it look red!

The different shapes of the Moon we see are called phases. When Earth is in between the Moon and the Sun, we can see a full Moon. When the Moon is in between the Sun and Earth, it's a new moon, which is invisible. In between these phases, it can be a crescent, gibbous or quarter moon.

Comets are big balls made mostly of ice that are too small to be planets, but still orbit stars like our sun. They have tails that we can see in the sky, which are caused by the Sun melting the ice and turning it into a gas.

Meteoroids are rocks that float in space. Sometimes these rocks travel through our atmosphere, where they will often burn up and turn into dust. When they burn, we can see a streak of light and they're known as meteors. Sometimes, the rock doesn't burn up completely and it makes it to the ground. The part that lands is called a meteorite.

You're not seeing the stars live! The stars you can see with the naked eye are so far away that it takes hundreds – or even thousands – of years to reach us. The bright light of a star you see in the night sky is the light that star gave off millennia ago, with the oldest stars we can see being around 4,000 years old.

Stars seem to appear white against the dark sky, but their actual colour depends on how hot they are. Blue stars burn at a heat of over 40,000°C and the coolest are red, but still reach temperatures of over 3,000°C.

It seems like it's impossible to count the number of stars when you look up at the night sky, but there are over 9,000 visible to the human eye. You won't be able to see them all at once, though, because the planet is facing away from half of them!

Not every light that you see in the sky is a star. Some of them are other planets in our solar system. You can see Mercury, Venus, Mars, Jupiter and Saturn at different times of the year, even without a telescope.

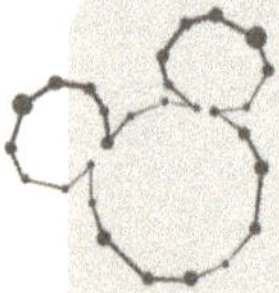

On very clear nights, you may be able to see part of the Milky Way galaxy that our sun is part of. It's a spiral-shaped galaxy and will look like clouds around the stars if you can spot it. These clouds are actually the dust and gases that surround the stars and planets.

Our moon isn't a sphere! It's shaped like a lemon, but the pointy bits face directly towards and away from us! Scientists think the Earth's gravity pulled it into this shape when the Moon was broken off from the planet hundreds of millions of years ago.

Scientists have dubbed the dung beetle the world's strongest creature. These insects can pull over a thousand times their own weight. That's like an average-sized adult pulling six fully loaded double-decker buses!

Insects called pond skaters live on the surface of still ponds and walk on water. Their bodies are designed to spread their weight over a large area, so there is never enough weight at any one point to break the water's surface tension.

There are over 20 quadrillion ants in the world, more than any other creature. That means there are 2.5 million ants for every person living!

Some insects have natural venom inside them to ward off predators. One clever bug, the red postman butterfly, creates its own poisonous brew by munching on toxic plants. Sometimes a clever instinct is stronger than any venom!

One of the hardest working insects is the busy bee. Its wings beat incredibly fast – around 230 times a second, or 13,800 times a minute. A single hive of bees can produce about 27 kilograms of honey per year, which is enough to fill 50 jars.

The Hercules beetle is one of the largest insects in the world, with adult males reaching 19 centimetres in length. But the most impressive thing about it is its strength – it can lift up to 850 times its own body weight! No wonder they named it after the powerful Greek hero.

When a bee find lots of pollen, she rushes back to her hive to tell the other bees by... dancing! She will perform a 'round dance' to let them know she's found a pollen-filled haven and a 'waggle dance' to tell them exactly how far away and in which direction it's in!

A water scorpion isn't actually a scorpion, as it has no sting in its tail. It lives mostly on land but crawls into ponds to hunt for food like small fish with its pincers. Its tail, rather than stinging prey, sticks out of the water and lets the water scorpion breathe underwater.

Insects have ears, but not like the ones you find on the heads of mammals. They often have hearing organs in strange places, like grasshoppers, which have them on their knees. That's like us having ears on our legs!

Insects generally don't live for very long, but they've been on Earth longer than humans. The oldest fossil containing an insect dates back over 400 million years, which was before even dinosaurs appeared on the planet.

Flying ants appear in a short season in the summer. The ones you see flying around are new queens and males looking to mate. Once a new queen has mated, she chews off her wings and seeks a spot to start a new colony by laying her eggs!

Lots of insects have compound eyes, which are made of several visual receptors in one body part that looks like an eye. A dragonfly has a compound eye that contains around 30,000 different visual units.

Some spiders don't spin webs at all, but they have other clever ways to catch their prey. Ground spiders shoot their webs at their prey to bind them and stop them moving, so they don't have to wait for their food to come to them.

The largest moth in the world lives in Queensland in Australia and has an average wingspan of around 27 centimetres, though the biggest measured 36 centimetres. This Hercules moth doesn't have a mouth to feed with, so it only lives for up to a week.

There are some insects that gardeners hate to see in their vegetable patch, but the ladybird is an exception. This colourful beetle eats aphids and other small insects that love to eat fruit and veg in gardens.

Spiders weave their webs from silk, which they create using an organ called a spinneret. The silk can be a thousand times thinner than a human hair, but scientists have worked out that it would be five times stronger than steel at human size!

It would be weird if you looked like a chip, wouldn't it? Or any food you ate for that matter. But in the insect kingdom, there's a bug called a phylliidae, or leaf insect, which eats plants and also looks exactly like a leaf, so carnivorous predators won't think it's food!

Humans have just over 600 muscles, which allow them to do incredible things with their bodies. The humble caterpillar, however, has over 4,000. They use these muscles to push blood between body segments and move each one up and down for movement.

Butterflies don't taste with their mouth, or anything on their face for that matter – they taste with their feet. This makes it easy for them to feed when they land on plants and other things abundant in nutrients that they need.

Scorpions give birth to live babies, unlike most insects and arachnids, which lay eggs. The baby scorpions live on their mother's back and live off a yolk sac until they're ready to strike out on their own, but some can live with their mum for up to two years.

Termites are not technically insects, but they're known for being wood-eating pests. It's no surprise when their colonies can grow so big – one termite queen was observed to pop out an egg every two seconds. The average queen can lay over 30,000 eggs in one day.

The heaviest bug in the world is the giant wētā, which is found only in New Zealand. It looks a bit like a cricket, but can't jump or fly because it's so heavy. The biggest giant wētā can weigh up to 70 grams, which is more than some mice.

Royalty in beehives works in mysterious ways. If a hive needs a queen bee, the nurse bees will pick one of the bee larvae and feed it a special substance called royal jelly, which turns the larva into a much bigger and more mature bee – the queen.

The bombardier beetle can ward off predators with a boiling hot chemical mixture. When threatened, it mixes these natural chemicals in its body and shoots them out at temperatures of around 100°C.

Ticks are found in grassy areas, usually in warmer seasons, and live off blood they suck from warm-blooded mammals. They can be as small as a seed when they're unfed, but can easily bloat to double or triple their size when they're full of delicious blood!

The biggest spider web ever recorded was spun by the Darwin's bark spider, which has the strongest silk of any spider. The web was over 2.8 metres square, but some silk lines measured over 24 metres!

Crickets can tell you how hot it is! A man called Amos Dolbear observed that if you count the number of cricket chirps you hear in 15 seconds and add 40, you'll get the air temperature in Fahrenheit. Amos came up with this method in 1897, so people have been using this method for over one hundred years.

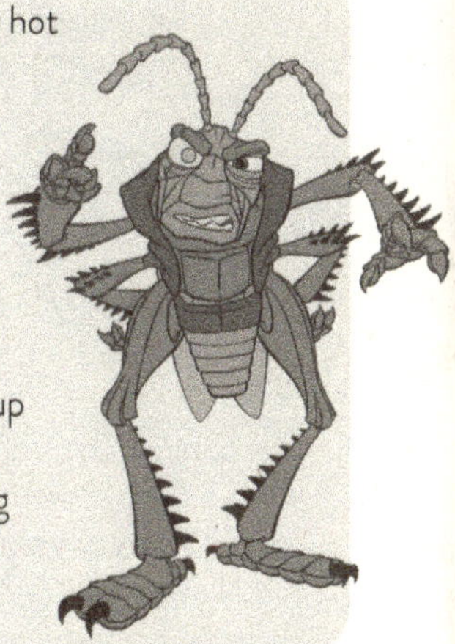

Spiders tend to avoid water, but the water spider loves to submerge in ponds and streams using a clever method. It captures air bubbles in its body hairs, then puts them inside a silk web. When the web is full of oxygen, the spider carries it around as an air supply, which lasts almost a full day.

The larvae of glow worms are natural-born killers. They inject toxins into the shells of snails or directly into slugs, which paralyse the poor creature and dissolve it into a liquid that the larvae suck up for nutrition.

You can find insects on every continent... but only just! There's only one species hardy enough to survive the frozen tundras of Antarctica – a wingless midge known as *Belgica antarctica*. Measuring up to just 6 millimetres, it's the largest solely land-based creature on Antarctica!

Cockroaches breathe through little holes in their bodies rather than through a mouth or nose as humans do. This means a cockroach can lose its head, but continue to breathe, move and live for a short time. However, it will eventually die as it can't eat any food.

Some ants will give their life for their precious colony. One type of exploding ant will detonate itself if a predator is attacking the colony, which coats it in a toxic liquid that either kills the enemy or slows it down so other ants can get away.

The common housefly can't chew food, so when it finds something it wants to eat, it vomits a pool of enzymes that break the food down into a puddle. The housefly then sucks up the nutrient-rich liquid and moves on to the next yucky meal.

One species of assassin bug has an unpleasant way of scaring off predators. It first hunts ants, which it uses for food most of the time. However, if it isn't hungry, it will stack the body of the ant on its back as a means of camouflage.

The largest family of insects is called the Coleoptera – or beetles to put it plainly. Scientists have discovered over 360,000 different species of beetle, from the humble ladybird to the gigantic Hercules beetle.

Aphids are all born female, and even more surprisingly, they're all born pregnant. Newborn aphids are known as nymphs, and will give birth just ten days after being born themselves!

The woodlouse, sometimes known as a pill bug, is usually grouped with insects, but is actually a crustacean, so it's more closely related to crabs and lobsters than ants and beetles. It can roll itself up into a ball when it feels threatened.

Not all insects are great for crops. The desert locust forms swarms of several thousand, and one locust can eat its body weight in a day – something humans only achieve in a handful of months! Locust swarms can cover up to 1,200 square kilometres and can contain between 40 and 80 million locusts per square kilometre.

The stick insect is known for its excellent camouflage – it disguises itself as a stick on plants and trees to avoid getting eaten. However, if a predator does see through its disguise, the stick insect can shed a limb to escape, which it can then regrow.

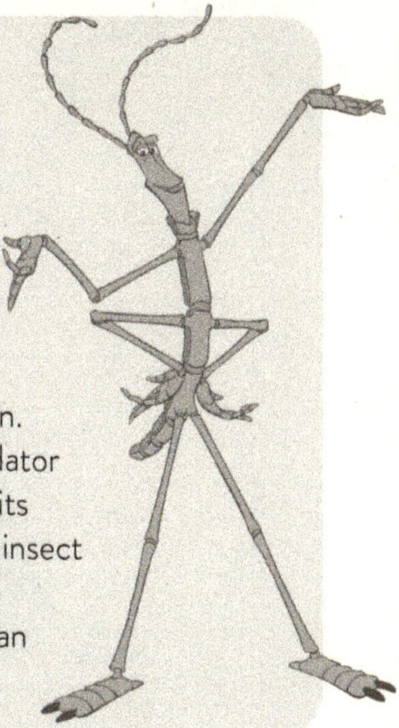

Some people see insects as pests, but they're super helpful! Pollinators like bees and butterflies are responsible for helping the spread and growth of 35 percent of the food crops that humans eat, as well as keeping 75 percent of wild plants alive.

Millipedes are thought to have a thousand legs, but this is a myth. They can have as few as 34 legs, although one species, the 3-centimetre long *Illacme plenipes*, has up to 750. That's more legs than any other animal on the planet.

Here's an earthworm you wouldn't want to find in your garden! The giant Gippsland worm can only be found in Australia and usually measures up to a metre long, although, the largest examples have been recorded at triple that size.

# THE ARTS

From the written word and most infectious music to the finest fashion and showstopping performances, the world of the arts is brimming with facts to get your creative juices flowing. Read on to find out some of the most unbelievable facts in the artistic world and be ready for inspiration to strike!

Charles Dickens was afraid of trains and with good reason too! In 1865, a train on which he was travelling dropped off a bridge. Although he was unhurt and returned to the crash to pick up his latest manuscript, he never went on another train.

France has produced more Nobel Prize winners in the field of literature than any other country in the world. Sixteen French people have received the honour to date, including Sully Prudhomme, the first winner of the award, in 1901.

The famous poet Lord Byron wasn't allowed to keep a pet dog while he attended Cambridge University, so he got another pet – a bear. He is believed to have purchased the giant mammal from a fair in the early 19th century.

William Shakespeare wrote at least 38 plays and 150 poems during his 52 years. No one is sure of the exact number because some may have been lost, and he might have had help from other writers with others.

In 1898, Morgan Robertson published a book called *The Wreck of the Titan: Or, Futility*, about a ship called *Titan* that hits an iceberg in the North Atlantic Ocean and sinks, with a shortage of lifeboats for the people on board. Fourteen years later, the *Titanic* sunk in exactly the same manner! Spooky.

Mary Shelley started writing her famous novel *Frankenstein* – the story of monster creation and its possibly more monstrous creator – when she was just 18 years old. She had the idea after a nightmare she had on a stormy night in Switzerland.

The first 'books' that combined words and pictures, and were read by children, were Japanese scrolls from as far back as the 12th century.

Samuel Pepys was an inhabitant of London in the 17th century who became famous for the diaries he wrote between 1660 and 1669. His personal accounts of the Great Fire of London and the Plague helped historians understand the events of the period.

The author of *Le Petit Prince (The Little Prince)*, Antoine de Saint-Exupéry, became a pilot during the First World War and rejoined the French air force when war broke out again in 1939. However, he went missing in 1944 while out on a mission.

Beatrix Potter first wrote an illustrated story about 'four little rabbits' to cheer up a friend's child while he was recovering from a bout of scarlet fever. She sent him the story to help him feel better and continued to write letters to him for many years until she published *The Tale of Peter Rabbit*.

The fastest-selling book in history is *Harry Potter and the Deathly Hallows*, which was the last book in the series. It sold over 8.3 million copies on its first day and went on to sell more than 30 times that amount across the world, in over 60 languages.

Quentin Blake, best known for being the illustrator on the books of Roald Dahl, has been the artist on over 300 different books. More recently he's illustrated books for David Walliams, such as *Gangsta Granny*.

The villain of J.M. Barrie's *Peter Pan* wasn't meant to be Captain Hook, it was meant to be Peter Pan himself! It started as a play before it was turned into a novel, but the stage crew needed more time to change sets, so a pirate scene was added in between scenes and Hook became the bad guy.

Aladdin in *One Thousand and One Nights* wasn't actually from the Middle East. The story begins with the words 'Aladdin was a little Chinese boy', although the collection of stories does have lots of influences from the Middle East.

*The Very Hungry Caterpillar* came from a piece of office equipment! Creator Eric Carle was playing around with a hole-punch and a stack of paper when he had the idea for the story about the insect with a big appetite.

A.A. Milne, the author of *Winnie-the-Pooh*, was taught by another famous author named H.G. Wells, who wrote *The War of the Worlds*. However, at that time Wells wasn't a published author and was teaching a maths class.

The monster in *Frankenstein* has no name – the doctor who made the monster is called Frankenstein! However, there is a part where author Mary Shelley has the monster refer to himself as 'Adam' when speaking to the doctor.

The only book printed in Latin to make the *New York Times* Best Seller list is *Winnie-the-Pooh*. The book was completely translated into the dead language and released as *Winnie ille Pu*!

The original edition of *One Thousand and One Nights* didn't actually contain the story of Aladdin! As well as 'Ali Baba and the Forty Thieves' and 'Sinbad the Sailor', 'Aladdin's Wonderful Lamp' was one of three stories that were added to later editions of the book.

The famous playwright William Shakespeare is thought to have invented hundreds of new words in his plays and other works. They contain the first instances of words such as bedroom, gloomy, puking and majestic.

Charles Dickens once founded a club dedicated to the investigation of paranormal activity. The Ghost Club was founded in 1862 by the *A Christmas Carol* author and other ghost-hunters of Victorian-era England, which might be where he got the idea for the ghosts in his festive novel.

One of the most famous writers of the 19th century, George Eliot, was actually a woman called Mary Ann Evans. She adopted the male pen name, which is known as a pseudonym, because she wanted to avoid stereotypes of women writing 'lighter' literature, like romances.

When it was published in 1865, Lewis Carroll's novel *Alice's Adventures in Wonderland* was banned in China because the animals talked. A governor in the Hunan Province thought that it was insulting to humans that animal characters could walk, talk and behave like them.

The most expensive book in the world cost $30.8 million! *The Codex Leicester* was written by Leonardo Da Vinci and contains only 18 pieces of paper, but that didn't stop Microsoft founder Bill Gates paying the massive sum.

All the profits that J.M. Barrie would have gained from the sale of *Peter Pan* were donated to the Great Ormond Street Hospital in London, which takes care of sick children from all over the United Kingdom.

L. Frank Baum, the author of *The Wizard of Oz*, named the fictional land in his story after a filing cabinet in his office. Two cabinets were labelled A–N and O–Z, and he was inspired to use the O–Z for an important part of his story!

One of the longest sentences in a novel is in *Les Misérables* by Victor Hugo at over 800 words long. From full stop to full stop, the sentence goes on for 823 words! However it only takes up 0.12 percent of the entire novel. Take a deep breath...

When he was still a schoolboy, Roald Dahl – who would later write *Charlie and the Chocolate Factory* and other children's classics – was a taste tester for Cadbury's. Sounds like the perfect research!

The longest novel ever written is *À la recherche du temps perdu* (*Remembrance of Things Past*) by Marcel Proust, which measures in at over 9.6 million characters – letters, punctuation marks spaces and so on – long. This equates to an absolutely gigantic 1.3 million words, so it'll take a while to read!

Lots of people love the smell of books, so it's not surprising it has a name – bibliosmia. The smell is caused by the chemicals used in the paper and ink of book production, and historians even use the presence of these chemical reactions to date old books!

The art of handwriting in an elegant style is called calligraphy. Historically, the Chinese valued calligraphy as an important skill, so much so that during the Tang dynasty, calligraphy was one of the skills needed to get a government job! Calligraphers would use a brush and black ink to write calligraphy. To make the ink, calligraphers rub an ink stick with water on an inkstone. Then they dip the brush in the ink and write the words on paper or silk.

Mexico is famous for the artistry of its painters, muralists and sculptors. The works of artists like Frida Kahlo, Diego Rivera, José Clemente Orozco, María Izquierdo and Sebastián have inspired millions. The Palacio de Bellas Artes, or Palace of Fine Arts, in Mexico City showcases artwork by Mexican artists.

You might think the Olympic Games are just for sporting achievements, but in the period between 1912 and 1948, competitors could enter events for architecture, painting and sculpture to win themselves a medal.

*The Starry Night*, one of Vincent Van Gogh's most famous paintings, was painted when he was a patient at Saint-Paul de Mausole Psychiatric Hospital. It shows the town of Saint-Rémy, which he saw out of his window.

Bas-relief artwork, which looks like it is raised from the wall, covers temples all over Southeast Asia. The pictures depict the history and well-known folklore of the region and the most famous examples can be found in Angkor Wat in Cambodia.

Using special chisels, Mexican artisans cut intricate designs into colourful tissue paper. Known as *papel picado*, this popular art form is often seen at celebrations and fiestas. People also use *papel picado* to decorate *ofrendas* during Dia de Muertos.

On many Pacific Islands, tattoos, like Maui's in *Moana*, were and still are a very important part of the culture – Samoans have been tattooing themselves for more than 2,000 years! These tattoos are done by hand, using a tool made from a sharp tooth or a row of metal teeth. Tattooing young men and women is a special, but very painful, event that is thought to show bravery.

Mexican folk art is unique in its use of intricate linework, vibrant colours, and fine embroidery. The region of Puebla produces a special type of painted pottery called Talavera. Tapestry artists in Oaxaca weave and embroider beautiful cloth and rugs. Shoppers in León and Guanajuato can find incredible leather goods for sale. In Jalisco and Nayarit, the Huichol people create detailed artwork with beads and yarn.

The indigenous people of Mexico have been creating art for thousands of years. Some examples from ancient times include cave drawings, murals by the Maya, and stone head sculptures by the Olmec. Aztec art includes decorated pottery, cloaks and headdresses woven from colourful feathers, and jewellery made from precious metals and stones.

Charles Darwin was born into a rich family and it's not surprising when you know who his great-grandfather was. Josiah Wedgwood was Darwin's great-grandfather and he was the founder of the Wedgwood pottery company that makes very expensive crockery.

The Musée du Louvre in Paris, France, is one of the biggest and most visited museums in the world. It's home to about 380,000 objects and displays 35,000 pieces of art, but that doesn't deter any of the 7 million people that visit every year.

The world's first animated film is over one hundred years old! *El Apóstol* (*The Apostle*), which was made in Argentina in 1917 arrived in cinemas 20 years before Disney's *Snow White and the Seven Dwarves*!

Michelangelo's incredibly lifelike sculpture *David* was supposed to be Hercules! Michelangelo took the marble meant for another sculptor, who intended to create the Ancient Greek legend, and spent three years carving his masterpiece.

Vincent Van Gogh wasn't famous while he was alive – in fact, he only sold one of his paintings in his lifetime, and even that was just before he died. Only after his death did people start to appreciate his art and his works started selling for millions of pounds.

Johannes Vermeer, a Dutch painter famed for his realistic scenes, has been accused of using a camera obscura to paint his scenes. A camera obscura is a light phenomenon where an exterior scene is projected onto a wall through a pinprick of light on an obscured window – some art historians think he basically traced his art!

A New York museum ran an exhibition featuring the paintings of Henri Matisse, but didn't notice that one painting, *Le Bateau*, was hung upside down for the duration. Luckily, the visitors hadn't noticed either.

Nobody knows who Banksy is! The graffiti artist has been painting pieces on walls across the United Kingdom since the early 1990s. They have made a film and have even run their own exhibitions, but still nobody has been able to work out who the mystery man or woman could be.

Salvador Dalí used to go to sleep dangling a heavy key over a plate so that when he went to sleep, the key would drop on the plate and wake him, allowing him to record his dreams, which he then used as inspiration for his surreal art.

It took Leonardo da Vinci three years to paint *The Last Supper*, but his most famous work – the *Mona Lisa* – took over five times as long! It's not surprising given how much time he spent sketching out inventions that were centuries ahead of their time.

The Sistine Chapel was originally meant to only contain paintings of Jesus's twelve apostles, but Michelangelo had bigger plans. He persuaded the Pope of the time to let him paint a bigger artwork, which now covers over 500 square metres of the Chapel's ceiling and contains over 300 characters.

Pablo Picasso was accused of stealing the *Mona Lisa* in 1911. A friend called Joseph Géry-Piéret sold a story to a French newspaper about stolen sculptures that Picasso had bought – even though Géry-Piéret was the one who stole them! Two years later, the *Mona Lisa* was found in Italy and Picasso was proven innocent.

Madame Marie Tussaud created life-size wax figures for the French aristocracy and was almost executed during the French Revolution, but was kept alive to make wax masks and casts of those who were sent to the guillotine! There are wax museums named after her all around the world today.

In 2001, a cleaner mistook the work of Damien Hirst for a pile of rubbish and threw it in the bin! In the cleaner's defence, it did consist of half-empty coffee cups, cigarette butts and sweet wrappers. Luckily, the piece was saved and reassembled within a day.

*The Story of a Ball* was created on the football pitch of Qatar University by Emad Salehi, an Iranian artist. It celebrates the history of football and the World Cup, which was held in Qatar in 2022, and is the largest art canvas in history, measuring over 31,666 square metres.

The *Mona Lisa* is so popular that the Louvre in Paris, where the painting is hung, has its own mailbox for all the love letters that she gets sent. People even send poems and flowers to da Vinci's famous painting.

Willard Wigan is an artist who focuses on making super-small creations. His tiniest work is a human embryo that was made from a carpet fibre, which was then placed inside a hollow piece of human hair. You need a microscope to view all of his works!

When statues were created in Ancient Rome, they were made with detachable heads. The sculptors made the modifications so if a general or emperor that was turned into a statue ever became a disgrace, they could take the head off and replace it with a new one.

Australia developed the first feature-length film in 1906, though most of it was destroyed. *The Story of the Kelly Gang* told the tale of legendary Australian outlaw Ned Kelly and it was thought to be lost to history until a few segments were found in 1976.

One of the first moving pictures dates back to the 1880s. It was created by a Frenchman called Louis Le Prince in 1888 and was a two-second clip of Le Prince's family dancing in the garden. It's known now as the Roundhay Garden Scene.

The first photograph was taken in 1826 using a camera obscura and a metal plate. The camera obscura projected the image onto the impressionable pigment-covered metal over eight hours and was made by a Frenchman named Joseph Nicéphore Niépce.

The most expensive photo sold at auction is called *Le Violon d'Ingres*, and shows the back of a woman with markings from a violin. It was taken by a photographer named Man Ray in 1924 and sold for a record $12.4 million in 2022.

*Venus of Willendorf* is one of the oldest sculptures in the world. It's around 10 centimetres in height and shows a rounded woman but nobody knows exactly what it was for. It was discovered in 1908 and dates back to at least 25,000 BC.

How many balloons does it take to float a house around the world? It's 10,297! Jon Reisch, the effects artist on *Up*, was in charge of the animation and revealed the massive number. Over 10,000 balloons were individually added to the scenes even though you can't see most of them.

The most viewed photograph is thought to be one of a green hill in California against a bright blue sky, known as *Bliss*. It was taken by Charles O'Rear and used as the default background image for users of Windows XP, which over 500 million people used every day.

Frida Kahlo, the legendary Mexican artist, almost became a doctor. At the age of 18, when she was just preparing to study medicine, she was in a bus accident that caused great injuries and led her back to the paintbrush. She created many self-portraits exploring the pains she had from the accident.

Louis Daguerre caught the first person on camera in 1828... by mistake! He was taking a picture of a road in Paris called Boulevard du Temple, but the exposure – the time it takes to form the photo on celluloid – took seven minutes and someone wandered into the street while it was happening.

Shadow puppetry has been around in Southeast Asia for generations. A candle is used to illuminate a screen, and puppets, traditionally made from leather, cast their shadows against it. Good puppeteers can make them appear to walk, talk, fight, dance and more. In Indonesia, shadow puppets are called *wayang kulit*.

Dance has been an art in China for over 2,000 years! A famous traditional dance is the dragon dance, where dancers dress as dragons and dance to ask for rain from the gods. Today, people perform this dance at celebrations and festivals. Multiple dancers hold a long dragon costume, creating movements that resemble flowing water.

The concheros dance includes steps from Aztec rituals. Dancers perform the steps to beating drums. They wear feather headdresses and colourful loincloths.

Danza de los Voladores means 'Dance of the Flyers'. Indigenous Mexicans created the dance centuries ago as part of a ritual to end a severe drought. To perform it, five people climb a 30-metre pole and then four of them jump. They dangle from the pole by rope tied around their ankles. The fifth person stays at the top of the pole and dances while playing a drum and a flute.

Zapateado is a Mexican style of dance similar to tap dancing, where the dancer's steps follow the beat of the music. The word zapateado comes from the Spanish word for shoe, zapato. Hector and Miguel dance in this style during the performance of 'Un Poco Loco' in *Coco*.

The witch in *The Wizard of Oz* wasn't given a name in the book, so when it was turned into the stage show *Wicked*, she was named Elphaba after the original author's initials: LFB for L. Frank Baum.

Lots of the biggest shows in theatre make it to Broadway, the famous theatrical street in New York, USA. Those that aren't as popular, are commonly known to be 'off-Broadway'; however, this is actually down to seating. Broadway shows have more than 500 seats in the theatre, off-Broadway shows have between 100 and 500 and off-off-Broadway shows have fewer than 100.

There's just one remaining double-decker theatre in the world: the Elgin and Winter Garden Theatre in Toronto, Canada. These theatres have two stages built on top of each other, with poorer attendees viewing the show on the lower stage, and the upper one hosting more wealthy theatre visitors.

During the time of Shakespeare, around the 16th and 17th centuries, women weren't allowed to perform on stage. All of the female roles in *Romeo and Juliet*, or *A Midsummer Night's Dream*, for example, had to be played by men!

The jarabe tapatío is the national dance of Mexico. It is a type of ballet folkorico, or Mexican folk dance. It's typically performed by a woman wearing a blouse and a wide, colourful skirt and a man wearing a type of dress known as charros, which is modelled after traditional horsemen. The dance features precise steps, quick turns and complicated skirt work.

*The Mousetrap*, a play based on an Agatha Christie mystery, is the longest-running theatre production in the world. It first played in London's West End in 1952 and has been running for over 60 years, celebrating its 28,000th performance in 2019.

Whistling backstage at the theatre is considered bad luck, as those who worked behind the scenes often gave cues with whistles. If someone whistled, they could accidentally give a cue for someone to do something at the wrong time during a show.

A ballerina called Pierina Legnani was the first to complete 32 spins on one foot – called a fouetté turn – without stopping. She performed the dizzying feat during the ballet *Cinderella*.

The longest round of applause for an opera lasted one hour and ten minutes! Spanish opera singer Plácido Domingo received that length of standing ovation for the title role in Giuseppe Verdi's *Otello* performed in Vienna in 1991.

It used to be illegal to perform the waltz! Critics in 18th-century Europe suggested that it was inappropriate to hold a dance partner so close and limited the amount of time waltzing to ten minutes, but the rules were relaxed in the early 19th century.

During the Baroque period (about 1600 to 1750), Spanish chapel masters taught their musical style to indigenous Mexicans. Indigenous music makers began to mix their music with Spanish and other European musical styles. This blend of European religious music with indigenous percussion instruments created a new style called Mexican Baroque.

There's a superstition in theatres that ghosts like to do their own shows, so some plays often take a break on Mondays to allow them to put these on. Most theatres leave a 'ghost light' on stage when they leave for the night so the ghosts can rehearse!

In the stage adaptation of Disney's *The Lion King*, around 230 puppets are used, ranging from shadow puppets to giant multi-person rod puppets. It took over 37,000 hours to make the puppets and the masks that the cast of the show wear.

In Indonesia, gamelan music brings together an ensemble, or a collection of performers and instruments. Instruments such as bamboo flutes, wooden keyboards, drums and gongs all combine to create a harmony. Gamelan is widely used in ceremonies, and you might also hear it in shadow puppet shows and other types of entertainment.

The oldest musical instruments discovered in China are flutes made from bone. These bone flutes are over 8,000 years old! Over time, the Chinese developed a variety of flutes, usually made from bamboo.

Son jarocho music began in the Veracruz region along Mexico's Gulf Coast. The music features indigenous, Caribbean and African influences. Common son jarocho instruments include the jarana and the requinto. These guitar-like instruments make a high-pitched sound. The arpa jarocha, or harp, is another main feature of this style. Miguel and Hector sing 'Un Poco Loco' in the son jarocho style in *Coco*.

For hundreds of years, indigenous Aztec and Maya people used instruments to create music. Early musicians made drums, rattles, whistles, trumpets and flutes from wood or clay. The Maya even crafted a special instrument using a drum, a string and sticks to mimic a jaguar's roar!

The famous rapper Tupac Shakur once took ballet! He attended the Baltimore School for the Arts, where he would have lessons in ballet, jazz and poetry among other subjects. He even had a lead role in the school's production of the ballet *The Nutcracker*.

Bamboo can sing! A khaen is an instrument made from a cluster of bamboo that is held together by beeswax. A musician uses a special circular breathing technique to create a continuous melody – it doesn't skip a beat.

The Christmas song 'Jingle Bells' is based on another song called 'One Horse Open Sleigh'. It was written for a sleigh racing event that happened in Massachusetts, USA – not during Christmas, but at Thanksgiving.

In Polynesia, a drum called the pahu is made from coconut trees and sharkskin. In Fiji, lali drums made from logs are common. In Papua New Guinea, many musicians played rattles made from seeds, leaves and shells.

The region in northeastern Mexico called La Huasteca gets its name from an indigenous group called the Huastec people. That's where son huasteco began. This music is known for falsetto singing and skilled violin playing. Son huasteco bands are often trios.

Banda bands started in the state of Sinaloa and can be found throughout Mexico. They often consist of brass, woodwind and percussion instruments. Banda includes a wide variety of music types, including waltzes, polkas, corridos and more.

What kind of instruments are played in the Pacific Islands? Some Polynesians play the nose flute. Other islanders play conch shells or panpipes. In recent times, the guitar and ukulele have become popular instruments to use in Pacific Island music.

Son jalisciense began in the west coast state of Jalisco in Mexico. Son jalisciense uses the vihuela, a small guitar, and the guitarrón, a large bass guitar. Violins, standard guitars, trumpets, and harps may also take part. Mariachi is the most popular form of son jalisciense music. A mariachi band plays during Ernesto de la Cruz's performance of 'Remember Me' in Coco.

Metallica are the only band known to have played on all seven continents. In 2013, they played a show on every single continent, including Antarctica, where they played to 120 people at the Carlini Base – most of the audience were scientists who lived there.

Over 60 years on from his prime in the 1950s and 60s, Elvis Presley remains the bestselling solo artist of all time. He's sold over 500 million records, and now that most people stream music, he's unlikely to be overtaken.

The oldest written music can be found on a gravestone in Turkey! The Seikilos Epitaph has lyrics and a musical composition carved into the stone, which dates back to the first century BC.

The largest rock band in the world contained 349 singers, 100 keyboard players, 151 drummers and 154 people shredding the guitar. In total, the Beijing Contemporary Music Academy band contained 953 musicians when they played a concert in 2016.

16th-century singer Orlando di Lasso became a talented musician and composer, but people loved his singing so much when he was young that he was kidnapped three times to sing in competing choirs.

The great composer Ludwig Van Beethoven wrote many famous pieces of classical music, but started to go deaf at the age of 28. When he lost his hearing, he bit down on a wooden stick connected to his piano so that he could feel the vibrations of the music he was playing.

John Cage was a composer who created a piece in 1952 called '4'33"' that was just 4 minutes and 33 seconds of silence. His intention was that an audience would just listen to the sounds around them and prove that anything could be music.

Japan has the shortest national anthem in the world and it contains only four lines. It's called 'Kimigayo', which translates as 'His Imperial Majesty's Reign', and takes around a minute to play from start to finish.

In 2016, on the 225th anniversary of his death, Wolfgang Amadeus Mozart was once again the bestselling musical artist in the world. He sold more CDs than popular artists such as Beyoncé thanks to a 200-disc special edition of his entire works.

There's an album consisting of music entirely recorded in space! Astronaut Chris Hadfield recorded all the tracks for *Space Sessions: Songs from a Tin Can* while he was onboard the International Space Station. The album was released in 2015.

Reggae music originated on the island of Jamaica in the 1940s, but it really took off in the 60s, when popular artists like Toots and the Maytals and Bob Marley exploded onto the scene and turned it into a genre loved around the world.

At St Buchardi church in Halberstadt, in Germany, an automated organ is performing a piece of music called 'As Slow As Possible', which will eventually end in the year 2640! The music was created by the composer John Cage and began in 2001, meaning it will last 639 years!

Traditional Chinese clothing is called hanfu. The term translates to 'clothing of the Han people'. Hanfu typically includes a shirt that crosses in front, a skirt or trousers, and a belt or sash. Shoes were usually made of black cloth.

The colour yellow was favoured by emperors from different Chinese dynasties. In fact, during the Tang dynasty, only the royal family was allowed to wear this colour. Emperors throughout the centuries also wore robes embroidered with dragons.

Most traditional clothing in Southeast Asia involves draping, which is the art of wrapping fabric into a particular shape. Sbai tops found in Cambodia, Thailand, and Laos are draped diagonally around the chest and cover the shoulders. Sampot trousers are wrapped around the waist, drawn between the legs from the front, and tucked in the back. Sarongs found in Indonesia are simply wrapped around the waist.

In Ancient China, people carried hand fans made from bamboo, silk, feathers or paper to cool themselves in hot weather. Foldable fans, brought to China from Japan, also became popular. Parasols, light umbrellas made of bamboo and paper, helped protect against the sun.

In Ancient China, people on farms and villages wore clothes made from cotton, linen or hemp fibres. Only the wealthy could afford clothes made from silk, which is a soft and light fabric made from the cocoons of silkworms.

Combs, like Mulan's lotus flower hair comb, were a popular accessory in Ancient China. Women wore them in their hair. The combs were often made of gold or jade. Jade is a hard stone that is usually green. It can also come in other colours like pink or white. In China, jade can be more precious than gold or silver.

Batik textile traditions of Indonesia and Malaysia use dye and wax to create repetitive patterns. In Laos and Thailand, handwoven silk textiles called brocade are sometimes produced from gold and silver threads.

Hats off to the nón lá! For over 3,000 years, this traditional Vietnamese conical hat has protected farmers in rice paddies from the elements. Today, many different versions exist throughout the region.

The Mexican sarape is a woven blanket worn around the shoulders by men and women. A rebozo is a large woven shawl or scarf that can be worn around the shoulders or the body. Sarapes and rebozos help keep the wearer shaded in the sun and warm at night. They go well with a pair of huaraches, or sandals.

China poblana is colourful, traditional clothing commonly worn by women who perform ballet folkorico in Mexico. It features a white blouse and red-and-green skirt. The china poblana is a Mexican national symbol.

A charro, or a Mexican horseman, wears tough and useful clothing like cowboy boots and a sombrero. The sombrero typically has a leather chin strap, so the hat doesn't fly off while horseback riding. The modern mariachi costume has its roots in traditional charro clothing, which is just like Ernesto de la Cruz's outfit in *Coco*.

The huipil is a loose-fitting blouse or dress with roots in indigenous Mexico. It is usually worn by women and allows air to flow through it easily, keeping the wearer cool on a hot day. A guayabera is a shirt with buttons usually worn by men that features two rows of carefully sewn patterns.

Some synthetic fibres are used to make flexible armour for people. The molecules of these fibres are made in a lab then spun into threads, before being woven into super-strong fabric used to make bulletproof vests and other protective gear. Super-strong synthetics include Kevlar, carbon fibre and Lexan.

Many early Pacific Islanders wore clothes made of tapa cloth. People from Fiji, Samoa, Tonga and many other islands made tapa out of tree bark. Villagers softened the bark by soaking it in water and beating it, and then decorated the tapa with beautiful designs.

Ancient Chinese armour was made of leather, bronze or iron and helped to protect soldiers from serious injuries in battle. The armour was layered like fish scales, which kept it from being too heavy and allowed soldiers to move more easily when they fought. Soldiers often wore helmets too.

The design of Mulan's armour was partly inspired by statues found in the tomb of Qin Shi Huang. These terracotta warriors were made to protect the emperor and serve as his army in the afterlife.

Many Pacific Islanders wear jewellery that their ancestors made from local island material. Shells, bone, seeds, wood and coconut are commonly used. Sometimes they wear it for special ceremonies, or to show wealth or power. Some kinds of necklaces are worn only by chiefs.

If you put your hands in the pocket of your jeans, you'll likely be able to feel a smaller pocket tucked inside it. It was originally intended to keep your pocket watch in, which is why it's – not surprisingly – called a watch pocket. Levi's have added it to their jeans since 1879.

White dresses weren't associated with weddings until Queen Victoria married Prince Albert in the 19th century. Before then, white was often a colour of mourning, but the Queen set a trend that's lasted for over a hundred years.

It's illegal to wear a fez – a small red hat with a black tassel on the top – in Turkey. They were banned in the 1920s because they were associated with the Ottoman Empire, which was a great rival of the Turkish people.

Both women and men of Ancient Egypt wore make-up because they believed it protected them from the sun and had magical healing powers too. They used natural materials like copper and lead to create the make-up.

Buttons on the sleeves of men's jackets weren't originally there to seal up the sleeve. Napoleon Bonaparte, the famous French admiral, ordered buttons to be attached to the sleeves so that his men wouldn't wipe their noses on their cuffs!

In the 17th century, the tsar of Russia Peter the Great, returned from a European tour and noted that most men did not have beards. He shaved off his beard and those of his court members and taxed anyone who wanted to keep their beards!

High heels were first worn by male horseriders in 10th century Persia (now Iran), when it was observed that the footwear helped riders to stay in their stirrups while shooting a bow. It was another 700 years before they became fashionable for women to wear.

The big airy ruffs that people wore around their necks in the 18th century weren't just for show – they were intended to increase ventilation for the wearer, who would often have many layers of heavy clothing. They were also thought to be used to wipe faces and keep them clean too.

Women in the 18th century often wore dresses lined with strong hoops to make wide cone-like shapes around their bodies. The pannier dress had special hoops that were very wide, turning women into walking walls, on which they could display their immaculately designed dresses.

Jeans are everywhere today, but do you know where they come from? Italy, or Genoa to be precise. The denim trousers that Genoan sailors wore were commonly called Genes, after the city where they were seen, which eventually changed to jeans.

In the late 19th century, European swimming costumes were super-heavy. Because showing any skin was frowned upon, women would wear long dresses made out of wool, as well as leggings, hats and underwear. It must have made swimming very hard!

Maria Paraskeva, a bride in Cyprus, broke the world record for the longest wedding veil in 2018. The lacy head covering trailed on for 6,962.6 metres. Hopefully the aisle she walked down was long enough!

The first fashion label to use a picture was Lacoste, which has a snappy green crocodile above the name. It first appeared in 1933 and represented the owner René Lacoste, who had gained the nickname 'the crocodile' during his tennis career.

# HISTORY

Turn the next few pages to begin a journey back in time! Walk with dinosaurs and gigantic animals that roamed Earth long before humans, take a trip across the world to see the ancient civilisations, and meet the people who created the world of today. There might even be a few myths sprinkled in too – they might not be true history, but they're amazing nonetheless!

Scientists think the age of dinosaurs probably ended with an asteroid impact at the end of the Cretaceous period about 66 million years ago. It killed all but a few of the dinosaur families – the relatives that remain today included crocodiles and birds.

Dinosaurs weren't the first complex creatures to walk the Earth. They were predated by reptiles called archosaurs and therapsids, which were the first animals to start living solely on land.

When the Triassic period began, the world wasn't split into continents like it is now. Instead, it was formed of one giant land mass known as Pangaea, so the dinosaurs really could roam across the world!

The Cretaceous period is named after the Latin word for chalk, 'creta', because the sea kept rising and falling in this time, killing lots of algae that fell to the sea floor. Over millions of years, this algae turned into the chalk we have today.

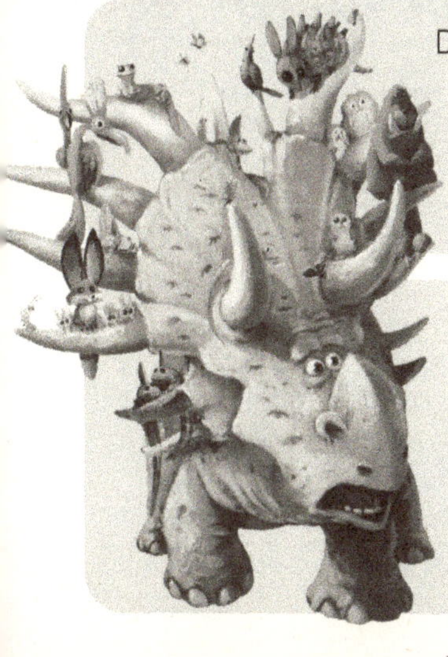

Dinosaurs first appeared in the Mesozoic Era, which was a period of time that began 252.2 million years ago! It's split into three smaller sections – the Triassic, Jurassic and Cretaceous periods.

At the end of the Triassic period, there was a series of massive volcanic eruptions, which caused an extinction event that killed off lots of land animals, though dinosaurs survived. The volcanic activity also split Pangaea into two separate continents: Laurasia and Gondwana.

Pterosaurs, like pterodactyls, aren't technically dinosaurs – instead, they're 'flying reptiles' from the Mesozoic Era. Creatures that lived in the oceans during the same era, such as pliosaurs and plesiosaurs, aren't called dinosaurs either, but 'acquatic carnivorous reptiles'.

The Parasaurolophus was a herbivorous dinosaur that had a big, bony crest on top of its head filled with tubes. Scientists think that it 'blew' these tubes to make really loud sounds to communicate with other members of its group.

The spiky plates on the back of a Stegosaurus are still a mystery to scientists today. They could measure up to 60 centimetres, but nobody is sure what they did – some think they were used to cool the Stegosaurus down, while others think they were used to scare away predators.

The biggest difference between the size of a dinosaur and the size of its brain is found in the Stegosaurus. These herbivores were the size of a van, but their brain was comparatively tiny – about the size of a lime!

The Eoraptor is the earliest known dinosaur that we've found so far, dating back around 230 million years. Its name means 'dawn thief' because it existed at the dawn of the dinosaur age. An Eoraptor skeleton was first discovered in Argentina in 1991.

If you thought swimming in the sea was scary now, give thanks you weren't around in prehistoric times! The biggest fish in the sea was a relative of a shark called the megalodon, which measured more than three times the size of today's sharks.

Palaeontologists – the scientists who study dinosaurs – often make mistakes when putting dinosaur fossils together. In the 19th century, one of them put the thumb bone of an Iguanodon on the end of its nose, while another connected the head of an Elasmosaurus to the end of its tail.

It's now widely accepted that dinosaurs weren't just the giant scaly lizards that we commonly think of – they were most likely covered in feathers! Some used them just for show, but others used them for warmth, or even to fly!

Not all dinosaurs were gigantic – one of the smallest known dinosaurs was the Microraptor and it would fit in the palm of your hand. It was a tiny carnivore that had feathers on its front and back legs that likely allowed it to glide around.

We're finding more dinosaur fossils now than ever before, at an average of one new species per week. Sometimes the fossils found by palaeontologists change what we think we already know about dinosaurs like the T. Rex.

By the time Tyrannosaurus rex – known as the 'tyrant lizard king' – was roaming the planet, the Stegosaurus was already a fossil. Though we often see the most famous dinosaurs together in fiction, the Stegosaurus had been extinct for millions of years!

The tallest dinosaur discovered is the Argentinosaurus, which was thought to reach a height of around 8 metres! It's also thought this dinosaur was the heaviest, estimated at around 82,000 kilograms – it would need to eat a lot to power that huge body after all.

Mary Anning was one of the first amateur palaeontologists, and discovered fossils around the beaches of Dorset, England, in a place now known as the Jurassic Coast. She was the first person to discover skeletons of marine reptiles like Ichthyosaurus and Plesiosaurus, before people even knew about dinosaurs!

The word dinosaur comes from the Greek words 'deinos' and 'sauros', which translates as 'terrible lizard'. They were given the name by Richard Owen in 1842, not because they're bad lizards, but more because they are massive!

There's a dinosaur named after the cast of the *Jurassic Park* film! The second part of the Tianchisaurus nedegoapeferima name includes letters from the surname of each actor – Sam **Ne**ill, Laura **De**rn, Jeff **Go**ldblum, Richard **A**ttenborough, Bob **Pe**ck, Martin **Fe**rrero, Ariana **Ri**chards and Joseph **Ma**zzello.

A childhood friend of Mary Anning's painted pictures of dinosaurs in Dorset to help raise money to fund her fossil-hunting. Henry De la Beche sold prints of Duria Antiquior, which showed artistic representations of Mary's discoveries around the coast of Dorset.

Most carnivorous dinosaurs would walk on two feet, which meant they were faster and kept their upper limbs free to attack their prey. The largest carnivore was the Spinosaurus, which could measure as much as 15 metres long, although it hunted in the water catching fish.

Two dinosaur fossil-hunters were engaged in The Bone Wars in the late 19th century. Othniel C. Marsh and Edward Drinker Cope raced to find dinosaur fossils around North America, which led to the discoveries of Elasmosaurus, Hadrosaurus, Diplodocus, Allosaurus and the Stegosaurus!

Scientists have discovered evidence that dinosaurs may have had fleas! Modern fleas feed on the warm blood of mammals, but scientists in China have found two species of flea with giant syringes which could be used to suck blood through the thick hide of a dinosaur.

The first dinosaur to ever be named was the Megalosaurus, which was a carnivore that could reach lengths of up to 9 metres. It was named by the British naturalist William Buckland in 1822 even before the word dinosaur was created!

Palaeontologists discovered a fossilised dino fight! The fossils are of a Velociraptor attacking a Protoceratops and it's believed their battle was interrupted by a landslide that covered and killed them both.

The first known fossil discovery dates back to 1677, when an English naturalist named Robert Plot came across a gigantic bone that he thought belonged to a giant ancestor of humans. It wasn't until dinosaurs were discovered years later when people realised it belonged to the ancient reptiles.

Lots of dinosaur fossils have been found with small rocks inside their rib cages, leading scientists to believe they are gastroliths – rocks swallowed to aid digestion. They've been found mostly in herbivores, but also some marine reptiles.

A palaeontologist and biologist named Hans Larsson is attempting to unlock dormant dinosaur traits in the DNA of their ancestors – birds. So far he has managed to get a chicken embryo to grow with the potential for teeth and a tail!

Scientists didn't know how dinosaurs reproduced until 1923, when an American explorer called Roy Chapman Andrews discovered dinosaur eggs in the Gobi Desert in Mongolia. The biggest dinosaur eggs we know of measured 30 centimetres, while the smallest fossilised non-avian dinosaur egg was smaller than a golf ball!

We know dinosaurs walked, ate and fought, but now scientists have discovered one that could kick. Brontomerus, which translates to 'thunder thighs', had an unusually large hip bone that could kick forward. It's the first time such a feature has been discovered in dinosaurs.

The spikes on the end of dinosaur tails – most commonly found in the fossils of the Stegosaurus – have a special name: a thagomizer. It was likely used as a weapon to defend itself, whacking any predators that attempted to come near it.

As well as being one of the most fearsome dinosaurs ever, the Tyrannosaurus rex can also claim the record for the longest dinosaur tooth! Each one of its 50 or so teeth could measure up to 25 centimetres long!

Over half of the dinosaur species that we know about come from a single specimen – which aren't always a full skeleton! Over 600 of the species we've discovered are based on just one skeleton.

Triceratops – which means 'three-horned face' has a relative that's a bit of a show-off. Rather than sticking with just a trio of horns, the Kosmoceratops has a whopping 15 horns attached to its giant skull!

There's a whole group of dinosaurs that are named after ostriches because they're so similar to the modern bird. Ornithomimids, or 'ostrich dinosaurs' all share long necks, legs and beaks with the ostrich we know today. One ornithomimid, Gallimimus, however, could be three times taller than a human!

Over 20 Tyrannosaurus skeletons have been discovered across the world. The most complete one is nicknamed Sue and was found in South Dakota, USA. Sue was sold at auction in 1997 for an amazing £5 million!

The Ankylosaurus was the dinosaur equivalent of a tank. It had bony spikes all along its back, up to its head and incredibly strong bony plates everywhere else. Its tail was like a gigantic club, which it swung at attackers to defend itself.

One of the longest dinosaurs ever discovered is the Seismosaurus, which had a length of over 36 metres. At that size, it probably had a pretty big stomp, which is why its name translates as 'earthquake reptile'.

With a long jaw resembling modern-day crocodiles and sharp teeth to match, the Baryonyx was thought to be a skilled hunter of fish. It also had claws on its thumb that could be used to impale slippery fish if they tried to get away.

The Apatosaurus's tail was so long and thin that some palaeontologists believe that it could behave like a whip and break the sound barrier if swished fast enough. That would mean its tail would move at a speed greater than 1,200 km/h!

The Mesozoic Era was the age of the dinosaurs, but after they became extinct, the world entered a new Era known as the Cenozoic Era. It started 66 million years ago and we're still living in it right now! It's sometimes called the age of mammals, as it's when these warm-blooded creatures began to dominate the Earth.

We humans used to share the Earth with other humanoid species including Neanderthals. They died out up to 40,000 years ago, but scientists have found evidence that they lived alongside us for thousands of years.

In 1940, four teenage boys were exploring the woods near the village of Montignac, France, when they discovered an unusual hole in the ground. When they entered the hole, they found a cave network covered with prehistoric artwork. These 20,000-year-old images shed new light on ancient peoples.

Stonehenge is a prehistoric monument in England that consists of a ring of large standing stones, each measuring about 4 metres high and weighing 22 tonnes. No one knows Stonehenge's original purpose for sure, but it may have been used for religious ceremonies. Many people believe that Stonehenge focuses earth energies in a magical way.

Tools have been discovered in Kenya dating back more than 3.3 million years! That's way before modern humans – or homo sapiens – were around, so they must have belonged to an even earlier species!

Dogs have been a human's best friend for more than 14,000 years. Though they'd be very different to the pets we have today, there's evidence that dog DNA started to differ from wolf DNA from the Stone Age!

The megatherium was a giant relative of the sloth that weighed as much as an elephant and was 6 metres long! It had bony plates under its skin that protected it from attacks and had massive claws to defend itself.

Early Celtic tribes in the British Isles would live in hill forts – massive fortified structures built around hills that would often encompass whole towns. These cropped up during the Iron Age when weaponry advanced so much that battles and wars became very common!

The earliest writing system that we have evidence of is called Cuneiform, which was found on tablets in what was once Mesopotamia, in the region that is now mostly Iraq. They date back to the Bronze Age, almost 6,000 years ago.

Medicine in the Stone Age wasn't quite as good as it is today– one method used was called trepanning, in which they would drill a hole in the skull to relieve pressure. One drilled skull found in Ukraine dates back over 7,000 years and we can tell that the person survived and made a full recovery!

The early recorded history of humanity is split into different ages based on common material – first came the Stone, then the Bronze, then the Iron Age. These ages started at different times depending on when the material was first used – for example, Turkey's Iron Age started around 1500 BC, while it didn't begin in England until 500 BC.

The last woolly mammoth was still stomping around Earth 900 years after the pyramids were built! The latest fossil of this ice-age beast was dated back to 1650 BC, while the last pyramid is believed to have finished construction around 2490 BC.

The humans of the Stone Age had to live through an ice age, which was when the world cooled down so much that most of the planet was covered in snow and sheets of ice. The last ice age ended just under 12,000 years ago, but had lasted over 100,000 years.

While the Neanderthals and humans – or homo sapiens – walked the Earth, there were two other human-like races that lived up to 2.5 million years ago. The first was homo habilis, which were the first humanoids to use tools, and homo erectus, who are said to be the first to use fire.

One incredible creature that went extinct during the Stone Age was the castoroides, which was a relative of the modern beaver. It was up to 2.2 metres tall, making it the size of a bear today, and had teeth measuring up to 15 centimetres long.

In the Stone Age, people wore the skins of animals. They would hunt lots of different animals for food and use the leftover skin to make warm covers for themselves.

Woolly mammoths first walked on the Earth over 300,000 years ago, but lived well into the Stone Age as they were hunted by the humans of the time. They're similar in size to the African elephant today, but were covered in a thick coat of fur that protected them from the cold.

The Smilodon, more commonly known as the sabre-toothed tiger, shared the land with mammoths and other huge animals of the Stone Age. It got its nickname from two massive teeth that it had in its upper jaw, which measured up to 28 centimetres in length.

The mammoth isn't the only extinct woolly mammal – there was also a woolly rhinoceros. This creature was a similar size to modern rhinos, but had a single gigantic horn that measured over a metre long.

Not all ancient animals that are relatives of today's creatures were huge. The Hyracotherium is a relative of modern horses, but was just the size of a dog. Scientists even think that it got even smaller as the world heated up millions of years ago.

Archaeologists have discovered a fossil in Kazakhstan that could belong to a unicorn. Well, they call it a Siberian unicorn and it's more closely related to modern-day rhinos, which isn't a surprise as they both have horns on their head. Unfortunately, it became extinct at least 29,000 years ago.

One of the largest flying birds ever discovered is the Argentavis, which had an estimated wingspan of 6.5 metres! It was so big that it would have found it hard to take off, so it likely lived in the mountains, where it could launch itself from high ledges to start flying.

The end of the Bronze Age saw humans combine two of their cleverest advances for a deadly purpose. They attached their newly tamed horses to carts with the trendy wheel to create war chariots that they rode into battle.

Though most of the giant beasts that roamed the world during the last ice age were mammals, Australia had the world's biggest lizard walking the land. Megalania was a relative of the Komodo dragon and could reach around 7 metres in length!

Cambyses II was a Persian king who had an ingenious plan for invading Ancient Egypt. He knew the Egyptians loved cats, so his army painted icons of the cat god Bastet on their shields and forced herds of cats ahead of them. The Egyptians didn't want to harm the cats or images of their god and surrendered the country to Cambyses.

Ancient Roman Gladiators were very expensive to train and feed. Some Romans would pay to own the sweat and muck scraped from a gladiator, which they used to moisturise their skin.

When an important Viking died, they would be placed in a burial ship rather than a tomb or a coffin. These ships contained all the Viking's worldly possessions and would be burned on their way out to sea, or covered in earth.

Queen Suriyothai of Thailand is famous for valiantly defending her husband during a battle against neighbouring forces in the 16th century. She is remembered for being a strong and immensely courageous leader. Monuments in her honour can be found in art throughout Thailand.

Raya's sword in *Raya and the Last Dragon* is inspired by a type of traditional dagger called the keris, or kris, found in Indonesia and Malaysia. It dates back at least 1,300 years and is famous for its wavy blade made from iron or steel, and is said to provide protection and good fortune to its owners.

The year 46 BC was 445 days long. Julius Caesar wanted to change the calendar that they were using to include a new month – July, named after him – but needed to also add in a few 'leap months' to keep the seasons aligned!

The era of Ancient Greece began in 323 BC, when Alexander the Great united the separate city-states of Greece. His Ancient Greek empire also included Egypt and parts of Southwest Asia.

Sisters Trưng Trắc and Trưng Nhị boldly led Vietnam's first major independence movement roughly 2,000 years ago. Highly skilled and strategic leaders, the sisters recruited an army of over 80,000 volunteers, many of whom were women. Today, they represent Vietnam's independence and are celebrated as heroes.

The Roman Emperor Caligula appointed an unusual senator while he ruled the empire. Partly because he loved the animal so much and partly because he wanted to embarrass other members of the Senate, he appointed his horse as a senator!

The Hanging Gardens of Babylon was a giant greenery-covered pyramid and one of the 'Seven Wonders of the Ancient World', thought to exist somewhere in what is now Iraq. Some believe it was built by the Babylonian king Nebuchadnezzar II for his wife, who missed the mountains and forests of her home.

Berserkers were a type of warrior Viking that wore animal skins – usually from a bear or a wolf – into battle and howled like animals to scare their enemies. It's where we get the word 'berserk' from today.

The Vikings beat Christopher Columbus to the American continent by around 500 years! They landed in what is now Canada around AD 1000, building settlements on the land before they eventually moved on.

The Ancient Greek tribes of the Medes and the Lydians were in their sixth year of warring when a solar eclipse occurred during a battle. They thought the eclipse was a bad omen, immediately stopped fighting and signed a peace treaty.

The Ancient Egyptian new year was called Wepet Renpet. In July, priests would watch for the reappearance of the star Sirius after a 70-day absence from view. They celebrated the new year when the star was visible, which meant that the Nile would soon flood.

Ancient Romans used to wipe their bum with a sponge on a stick instead of toilet paper! A philosopher named Seneca wrote about the invention – called a tersorium – over 2,000 years ago. Between uses, it's believed to have sat in a bucket of vinegar or salt water.

Alexander the Great of Macedon was an Ancient Greek leader who won his first battle at the age of 18! In fact, he never lost a battle in his whole life and created an empire spanning much of Europe and Asia. He was also educated by the famous philosopher Aristotle from the age of 13.

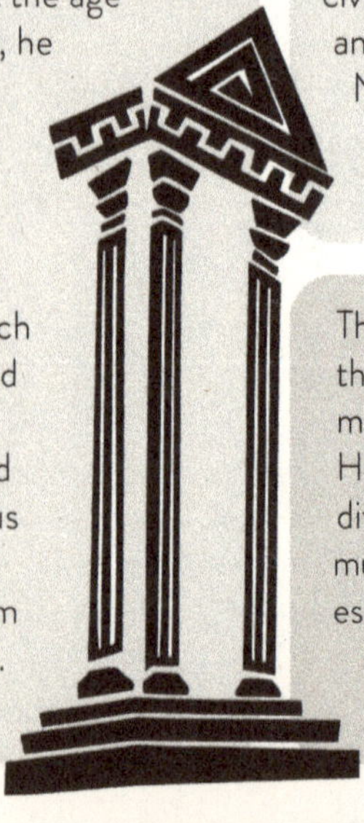

The oldest complaint letter that we know of dates back around 4,000 years. It's from the ancient civilisation of Mesopotamia and came from a man called Nanni, who was complaining about a batch of copper that he'd bought.

The word gladiator comes from the name of the short swords that most of them used: the gladius. However, there were many different gladiator types, including murmillones who used shields, essedarii who rode in chariots and retiarii, who used a net and a trident.

More than 4,000 years before the mummies were being made in Egypt, the Chinchorro people of Chile were mastering mummification. They removed the organs and muscles from the body and replaced them with plants!

There's evidence that the people of Ancient Rome used wee as mouthwash! They didn't have the minty fresh liquid we have today so they used urine as it contains ammonia, a natural and strong cleaning chemical.

Archaeologists have discovered a skull in Germany that is so well-preserved, it still has its hair attached! It's known as the Osterby Man and is thought to date back to between AD 75 and 130. It was found in a bog that helped to keep the hair intact.

Have you ever seen a dog wear a spiked collar? Well they were invented by the Ancient Greeks, not because they looked cool or tough, but because the metal spikes would stop wolves from killing the sheepdogs of farmers.

Ancient Greeks used two poisonous elements to dye their hair! They combined lead and sulphur, both of which are harmful to humans, when they wanted to change their hair colour, even though they can cause all sorts of damage – including death! Some modern hair dyes still contain toxic ingredients.

Over 2,000 years ago in the deserts of Peru, there were a group of people called the Nazca, who etched the rocks with giant images. These Nazca lines show different animals and are so huge they can only be seen from mountains or when in flight.

Engineers in Persia, which is now Iran, were able to create giant freezers that could store ice during their boiling hot summers. The ice was collected from mountains nearby during the winter and placed in a Yakhchāl, which was a giant dome building with an underground section that cleverly remained cool.

The earliest person that we know the written name of lived in Ancient Mesopotamia, around 3200 BC. His name was Kushim, an accountant who signed a receipt with his name confirming how much barley someone had received that year!

The Circus Maximus in Rome is another stadium like the Colosseum; however, this was exclusively used for chariot battles. It held races for Ancient Roman emperors like Augustus from 50 BC and could hold crowds of over 150,000 people – more than most stadia today.

Off the coast of Scotland, on the island of Orkney, there's an ancient village called Skara Brae, which was occupied during the late Stone Age, between 3180 BC to 2500 BC. It's one of the most well-preserved ruins of its kind due to the isolated nature of the island and the fact it was covered in sand until AD 1850.

Ancient Incans lived around 2,000 years ago, and developed a technique that made their buildings resistant to earthquakes! Their builders used irregular stones to lock in solid connections and even when the buildings moved during a strong quake, the stones would slide into their original position again!

The Ancient Greeks used slings to throw stones at their enemies and archaeologists have found that they sometimes carved messages on these rocks before flinging them. There's one at the British Museum that has a message that translates to 'catch!' etched on its side!

Three British kings may have died while sitting on the toilet! Some accounts suggest King Edmund II passed away on the porcelain throne in AD 1016, and 200 years later King John met his end on – or at the very least near – the loo. The last one rumoured to suffer the embarrassment was King George II in 1760.

King Henry VII had staff in his home called 'grooms of the stool', who would help him out in the toilet – including wiping his bum! It all paid off eventually as the pampered king later knighted anyone who had held the position.

Pocahontas was a real person! She was the daughter of the Powhatan Chief, who led the Powhatan nation in the region of the USA that's now Virginia. Her real name was Amonute, and she also had the more private name Matoaka, but she was given the nickname Pocahontas, which means 'playful one', when she was young.

Mary, Queen of Scots was made the ruler of Scotland aged just six days old! Her father, King James V died just a few days after she was born, but Mary was the only heir. Fortunately, somebody else made the decisions until she was old enough to do so herself!

Pope Gregory IX, leader of the Roman Catholic church in the 13th century, declared that cats were related to the devil and should be killed! He was the leader of one of the world's biggest religions, so Catholics listened, and it's thought that the lack of cats contributed to the spread of the plague by undisturbed rats!

Henry VIII is famous for having six wives during his life, but he only divorced two of them. It turns out that they were the lucky ones – two of his wives, Anne Boleyn and Catherine Howard, were beheaded!

The fearsome pirate Blackbeard was an Englishman by the name of Edward Teach. He sailed the seas of the Caribbean during the 17th and 18th centuries. He would set light to cords placed under his hat before he attacked ships so it looked like he was spewing smoke from his head!

The Black Death killed around a third of the European population during the Middle Ages and it's all the fault of rats. The rodents carried a disease called the bubonic plague, which spread to humans via fleas. Over 75 million people died from the plague across the continent.

The Great Fire of London raged through the capital city's streets for four whole days in 1666, nearly razing the city to the ground! It spread all over London and destroyed many landmarks including St Paul's Cathedral.

A plague of dancing hit Strasbourg, France in 1518 and nobody knows what caused it! Over 400 people were thought to have been bitten by the dancing bug and some even died from exhaustion.

One of the richest men to ever live was an African emperor called Mansa Musa, whose reign spanned the 13th and 14th centuries. He was the leader of the West African Mali Empire and historians estimate his fortune to be worth billions of dollars today.

Napoleon is one of the most famous generals in history, but he struggled against one foe: rabbits. He organised a rabbit hunt in the early 19th century, but when the thousands of bunnies were released, they swarmed and attacked Napoleon and his hunting pals!

In Medieval Germany, a married couple could settle disputes with a marital duel, which was basically a fight to settle a legal argument. The man had to have one hand tied behind his back and be standing in a hole, while the wife had a bag of rocks to wield!

A monk and philosopher in the 13th century came up with the idea of cars and planes long before people actually managed to make them. Roger Bacon believed that vehicles could be made 'so that without animals they will move with unbelievable rapidity' in a time when horses were still pulling carriages.

Torture was common in Medieval times, but the Iron Maiden wasn't. The coffin filled with spikes that was said to be slammed on people was invented by a museum curator when he added sharp spikes inside an old sarcophagus!

People used spoons and knives in the Middle Ages instead of using forks. Many men believed forks were too feminine, which meant they didn't catch on for a long time.

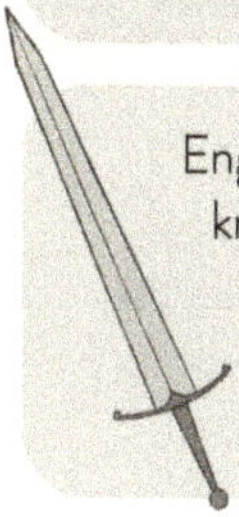

English drivers travel on the left side of the road because of the knights in Medieval times. Most knights were right-handed, so when they rode their horses, they rode on the left side of a road or track to keep their sword hand on the side of any passing enemy.

Would you let a barber operate on you? Well, in the Middle Ages, barber-surgeons were quite common as they had the delicate cutting skills required to cut hair or perform surgery. The spinning red and white poles at some barbers represent the blood and bandages that they dealt with.

Many towns in Eastern Europe were afraid of vampires in the Middle Ages. Archaeologists discovered a 13th century skeleton in Bulgaria that had been staked through the heart, presumably as the townsfolk thought he was a vampire!

Animals could be convicted of crimes in the Middle Ages. The most common suspect was the humble pig – there are dozens of records of them being tried for crimes like stealing food and eating body parts. The court of Marseille even put a pod of dolphins on trial in 1596.

Doctors in the Middle Ages had some unusual procedures to help their patients. They'd use leeches on wounds to suck out dirty blood and clean them of infection instead of cleaning and stitching wounds like they would today! Although in certain, very specific medical situations, leeches can still be used today to save life and limb.

In AD 1252, King Henry III of England was given a polar bear as a gift from the country of Norway. He kept it locked up in the Tower of London, but let it out to hunt for fish in the River Thames!

Though they're usually shown with horns on their helmets, Vikings probably didn't have the pointy attachments on their headwear as they would be too easy to knock off. It's thought that costume designers for plays and operas in the 19th century added the horns to make more interesting outfits.

Football has existed in England since as far back as the 14th century, though it was drastically different to how it is played today. There was no limit to the number of players – you could kick the enemy team and it was often played across entire villages. No wonder King Edward II banned it in 1314!

In 1872, the crew of the ship *Dei Gratia* happened upon another ship in the Azores. It was called the *Mary Celeste* and it was abandoned in the middle of nowhere – over 600 kilometres from land. All the former crew's possessions were on board, but it was a ghost ship.

During World War II, the British government covered the precious landmark, the Taj Mahal, in bamboo. They hoped that if they disguised it as nothing more than a bamboo stockpile, enemy bombers either wouldn't see it or wouldn't think it was worth destroying.

The shortest war in history started on 27 August 1896... and finished on the same day! The Anglo–Zanzibar War between Britain and Zanzibar lasted just 40 minutes and resulted in a victory for the Brits.

A Japanese soldier sent to the Philippines to spy on the Americans during World War II didn't find out that the war had ended until almost 30 years later, in 1974! Many people tried to tell him, but he thought it was a trap until his retired boss flew to the Philippines to tell him.

Mahatma Gandhi was an Indian activist who helped the huge country gain independence from Britain in the 20th century. He used a method called satyagraha, which involved peaceful protests against the ruling colonists rather than violent means.

Abraham Lincoln, the 16th president of the United States, was a champion wrestler before he took the nation's most powerful seat. He had taken part in over 300 bouts and lost just once out of all of them!

During the Industrial Age and well into the 20th century, some people in countries including Britain, Ireland and the Netherlands, employed a knocker-upper to get them up for work instead of an alarm clock. They would walk along the streets and bang on the windows of people they needed to wake with a stick, or by firing a pea shooter.

The Suffragettes were a group of women in the UK who protested for change to the laws of the land that would allow women to vote. Women like Emmeline Pankhurst led the movement with headline-grabbing – and sometimes dangerous – protests, but all women over the age of 21 finally gained the right to vote in 1928.

To stop Paris from being bombed in World War II, France constructed an almost identical version of its capital city using wood and canvas. They used French fighter planes to note what was most visible from the skies and fool the enemy combatants. However, the war stopped shortly after the fake Paris had been finished!

The *Titanic*, which tragically sank in 1912, was actually called RMS *Titanic*. The RMS stands for Royal Mail Steamer, so as well as the guests, the ship was also carrying over 3,000 letters and packages destined for North America.

On Christmas Day in 1914, which was during World War I, British and German soldiers stationed near no man's land agreed to a truce to mark the special day. They shared food, talked and even played a football match with each other.

In 1919, 12,000 metric tons of molasses surged through the streets of Boston at 56 km/h – the result of a tank container bursting. It was a giant sticky tidal wave that apparently reached up to 4.5 metres and killed 21 people.

Until Queen Elizabeth II, the longest-reigning British Monarch was Queen Victoria. She became queen in 1837 and her rule lasted over 60 years of the Industrial Revolution until she died in 1901. Luckily, she had nine children ready to take over from her.

In the Great Depression, when poverty was at its highest, flour manufacturers started to make their sacks out of colourful cloth so that people could make clothes out of the sacks to save money.

As a 'conductor' on the Underground Railroad – a series of safe stops on the way to the free north of the United States – Harriet Tubman led hundreds of enslaved people to safety. She even continued her work when the American Civil War started in 1861.

After the *Titanic* sank, it took 73 years for someone to find the wreckage again. In 1985, an oceanographer named Robert Ballard found a shipwreck 600 kilometres away from the coast of Canada. He explored underwater using a submarine called *Argo* and discovered the legendary *Titanic* on the ocean floor.

Florence Nightingale was born to wealthy English parents in Florence, Italy – which is where she gets her name – so she didn't need to get a job. However, she believed it was her calling to become a nurse. Florence became a hero of the Crimean War in the 19th century, and is credited with cleaning up medical facilities of the era.

When Rosa Parks was refused a seat at the front of a bus in the United States, Martin Luther King Jr organised a boycott of the bus company that lasted 381 days. After a year of peaceful protesting, local courts started to debate their laws on segregation – the separation of Black and white people – in a major victory for the civil rights movement.

Alan Turing led a team of codebreakers at Bletchley Park, England during World War II. They developed a way to translate the Enigma code that the Germans used to send messages, which some experts say turned the war in the Allies' favour and shortened it by up to two years!

The British Army hired a magician during World War II to pull off clever illusions. Jasper Maskelyne helped the army invent ways to deceive the enemy including inflatable tanks, hiding weapons in sports gear and clever camouflage.

When the British Army were planning the D-Day landing in Normandy, they appealed to members of the public for postcards of Europe so they could analyse the pictures on them and choose the beach that was the hardest to defend.

The British Royal Family is German! Queen Victoria was the daughter of a German princess, Victoria of Saxe-Coburg and married Prince Albert, another German. The Queen also had a German governess looking after her as a baby and only spoke German until she was three years old.

Nelson Mandela, the South African freedom fighter and later president, was born to royalty! His father was a chief of the Thembu royal family and grandson of the king, but Mandela still blazed a trail as a human rights activist in the African nation.

When the Berlin Wall fell in 1989, it happened a lot quicker than it was meant to. A politician mixed up his words and said that Germans could pass along the border between East and West Germany 'without delay', which caused thousands to flock to the wall, charge through checkpoints and eventually tear the wall down!

Aztec myth says the god Huitzilopochtli (weet-seeloh-POHCH-tlee) claimed his people would know where to settle when they saw an eagle eating a snake while perched on a nopal cactus. After wandering for weeks, the people finally saw the eagle in a large marsh. They founded Tenochtitlan (teh-nohch-teet-LAHN), the capital of the Aztec Empire, which is now Mexico City.

The kraken is a legendary Scandinavian sea monster. This enormous octopus-like creature is said to lurk in the waters off Norway and Greenland, terrorising sailors and their ships. Unlike many mystical beings, this one may be based on a real creature like the giant squid.

In *Coco* Miguel's great-great-grandmother, Imelda, sings a popular Mexican song called 'La Llorona' at the Sunrise Spectacular. The song is partly inspired by the legend of the Weeping Woman, La Llorona, who cries as she searches for her lost children. Bad luck may strike anyone who crosses her path.

Tengu are magical creatures from Japanese tradition. If they get angry, they can cause raging storms and form whirlwinds that carry people into the air. They are also forest guardians who get upset if trees are damaged, but woodcutters can soothe them with offerings of food.

An ancient story tells how Popocatépetl (Popo) was in love with Iztaccihuatl (Izta), a princess. A jealous rival told Izta that Popo died in battle. When Popo returned, Izta had died of a broken heart. He built her a monument and stood guard over her body. Eventually, both were covered by snow and transformed into volcanoes. When smoke rises out of El Popo, it is evidence of his heart's eternal burning love.

In African mythology, Ọya is the goddess of the wind, fire and thunderbolts, who also guards the gates of death. She is strong, brave and always willing to take risks. When she is angry, she may create tornadoes and hurricanes.

Mulan is an important heroine in Chinese culture. Historians think her story was first written by an unknown poet over 1,400 years ago. The story tells of a daughter who disguises herself as a man and goes to battle in her father's place.

Sisu and her siblings from *Raya and the Last Dragon* are inspired by the mythical nāga, a water dragon that protects rivers, lakes and oceans. These demigods have great powers, such as shape-shifting and providing rain. In the Philippines, they are called the Bakunawa, in Malaysia, the Seri Gumum and in Laos and Thailand, the phaya nak.

Traditional Chinese calendars are organised in 12-year cycles, with a different animal representing each year. An ancient myth explains how the Chinese zodiac came to be: The Jade Emperor invited all animals to race to the Heavenly Gate to be his guards. The first twelve to finish would be honoured with a place in the calendar. At the end of the race, the ox helped carry the rat across a river, but the rat jumped off the ox at the finish and earned first place.

Māori are the indigenous, or native, people of New Zealand, and many myths feature Maui, who is also a character in *Moana*. In one, he uses a magic fishhook to pull the North Island of New Zealand from the sea, while he stands upon the South Island. That's why the North Island's other official name is Te Ika-a-Māui, the great fish of Maui.

In Hawai'i, there are many legends about Maui. One says he made the sun slow down so that the days would be longer. Another says he lifted the sky with his arms. A third says that he discovered the secret of fire and gave it to people.

The people of Finland say the Northern Lights come from a fox made of fire. The fox runs on the snow in the far north and when it sweeps its tail, sparks fly up in the sky. That's why the Finnish call the Northern Lights 'fox fire'.

In Polynesia, people worshipped many gods. They called them akua. Maui is just one akua of many. There is also Kanaloa, god of the ocean. There is Kine, god of creation, sunlight and freshwater. There is Lono, god of farming and rain. Each akua is in charge of a different part of life.

In Māori myths, the sky father Ranginui and the earth mother Papatūānuku held each other so tight that their children were forced to live in the darkness between them. Then one of their sons, Tāne, the god of the forests and birds, pushed his parents apart – and let the light in. To this day, Ranginui and Papatūānuku are sad about being separated, and the rain and mist are their tears.

According to legend, the Mycenaeans of Ancient Greece took over the city of Troy in 1180 BC with the help of a giant wooden horse. The soldiers hid in the horse, which was left outside the gates of Troy as a gift. When they wheeled it in, the soldiers took over the city!

The Ancient Egyptians worshipped over 2,000 different gods! Each of them was said to be in control of a different facet of life. Ra was the hawk-headed god who brought the sunrise, while Bes looked after mothers and babies.

The legend of how Rome was born begins with two abandoned brothers: Romulus and Remus. They were raised by a she-wolf in the spot where Rome is now, but Romulus killed Remus when they were adults and became the first ruler of Rome.

Hercules, also known as Heracles, was the demigod son of Zeus, the ruler of Mount Olympus, and a princess. His brother ruled Ancient Greece and set Hercules a series of 12 labours, which had him fight a nine-headed hydra and a giant lion, as well as capturing a minotaur and Cerberus, the three-headed dog that guarded the underworld.

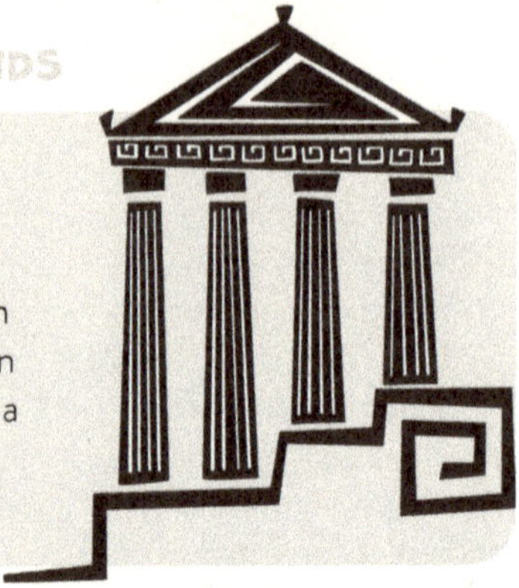

In Greek mythology, King Theseus defeated a minotaur that had been demanding children as sacrifices. He descended into the minotaur's labyrinth and slayed the beast, saving the children that remained. Clever Theseus had left a trail of string from the entrance so he could easily escape too.

The Vikings of Scandinavia had their own pantheon of gods that they worshipped, from Thor, the god of thunder and son of Odin, to Loki, the mischievous trickster god, who could shapeshift into the form of any animal.

Medusa is a creature of Greek mythology called a gorgon – she had snakes for hair and a stare that turned anyone who looked at her into stone. The fighter Perseus agreed to vanquish Medusa for his king, and used his shield to spot her without meeting her gaze, then defeated her.

The Norse gods lived in Asgard, a realm separate from the land humans inhabit, which they called Midgard. There were seven other realms, including Jotunheim – the land of the frost giants – and Hel, the realm of the dead.

Ancient Egyptians believed that the River Nile was the path between life and death. They thought that as the sun set in the west, it meant death, or the end, so they built all their pyramid tombs on the west of the Nile too.

The first mention of King Arthur was written in a Latin text called *Historia Brittonum*, but members of his Round Table, like Merlin, were first found in the most famous Arthurian text, *Historia Regum Britaniae*.

Even gods have parents! Ancient Greek god Zeus was the son of Cronos and Rhea, who belonged to a group of super-gods called the Titans. Cronos used to swallow all of his children because he was told one would overthrow him, but Rhea replaced Zeus with a rock when he was born.

When Hercules died, the Olympians honoured him by turning him into a constellation so he'd continue to live among the stars. You can still see him today – he's the fifth biggest constellation in the Northern Hemisphere.

If Ancient Greek legend is to be believed, Hephaestus the blacksmith god created the first robot. It was a bronze automaton called Talos and filled with ichor – the blood of the gods – which gave it its power. Zeus ordered it to protect the island of Crete, where it would throw boulders at ships.

The Golden City of El Dorado is a tale based on the Muisca people of Colombia. It stems from the ceremony of choosing a new leader, who would be covered in gold dust and given gold items that he would then throw off a raft in the middle of a lake as an offering to the gods.

Japanese folklore is filled with spirits called Yōkai, which cause trouble for the people of Japan. One of the most famous ones is a giant catfish called Namazu the Earthshaker, which lies underground and thrashes around to create earthquakes when not watched by the god Kashima.

Romans would be buried with a coin to pay their way to the underworld when they died. The coin was used to pay Charon, the ferryman, to row them down the River Styx to the realm of Pluto, the god of the dead.

# SCIENCE

It doesn't matter whether scientists are looking inside your body or to the far reaches of the universe, incredible discoveries are being made every day in the world of science. Now it's your turn to explore amazing facts, from the laws of robotics and dwarf planets to the atoms that make up you, the Earth and everything in the cosmos!

Our solar system has eight planets orbiting around its star, the Sun, but there are some planets that don't orbit a star at all. Scientists call them 'rogue planets' and they just float through interstellar space on their own. Some estimate there could be up to 200 billion rogue planets in our galaxy alone.

The first spacecraft, *Sputnik 1*, was launched into space in 1957. Since then, thousands of craft have blasted off into the great unknown, though only a few have carried humans. Astronauts have orbited our planet and travelled to Earth's moon and someday soon, spacecraft may take explorers to Mars and beyond.

A company called Mars One planned to build a human colony on the planet Mars by the year 2032 and over 4,000 people signed up to leave their whole world behind forever. But Mars One went out of business in early 2019, so these adventurers will have to wait for their Martian voyage.

Humans have barely scratched the surface of outer space. In the future, probes and human-accompanied expeditions will continue to explore. Technologies based on Earth, such as telescopes and spectroscopes that sense wavelengths invisible to the human eye, will also help scientists learn about our universe.

Enceladus, one of Saturn's moons, is dotted with ice geysers. These geysers spew water vapour from deep beneath the moon's surface. The vapour freezes instantly when it leaves the ground. The frozen crystals blast into Enceladus's atmosphere, where they form an icy ring. *The Incredibles*' Frozone would be proud!

Space is completely silent. Sound travels on vibrations in the air, but space is what's known as a vacuum – it has no air or atmosphere. Astronauts have to use radio wave communication so that they can talk in space.

Some of our solar system's planets are greedy with moons. Whereas Earth only has one moon, Saturn has 146 natural satellites that we know of. Its biggest moon, Titan, is bigger than Mercury.

Venus rotates on its axis so slowly that one day there is equivalent to 243 days on Earth. However, it only takes Venus 225 Earth days to orbit the sun, meaning the Venusian day is longer than a Venusian year.

Between Jupiter and Mars, there's a huge field of asteroids known as the asteroid belt. It contains millions of floating asteroids. The largest object, Ceres, is 952 kilometres wide. It's so big that it's classed as a dwarf planet, just like Pluto.

Earth isn't the only planet that has volcanoes. In fact, if you travel just one planet along to Mars, you'll find a volcano called Olympus Mons, which is over 600 kilometres wide and 21 kilometres tall. It's almost three times the height of Mount Everest and scientists think it could still be active.

Researchers at Yale University think they've discovered a very pricey planet. It's called 55 Cancri e, is twice the size of Earth and is possibly formed of diamond. Unfortunately, it's 40 light-years away, so we can't visit it to pick up some precious gems!

The hottest planet in our solar system isn't the one that's closest to the Sun! The temperature on Venus can reach 450°C (232 °F), helped by its super-thick atmosphere, which retains heat. Mercury has no temperature-regulating atmosphere, so its heat fluctuates more.

The Sun generates energy by converting hydrogen into helium, which increases its mass. When its mass increases enough, it will be classed as a red giant star and it will expand to reach Mars, swallowing Earth in the process. Don't worry, it will take another five billion years to reach us!

Jupiter is composed of the same elements as our sun – hydrogen and helium – so it has all the ingredients to be a star. However, even though it's the largest planet in our solar system, it would need to be at least 80 times bigger to start burning.

Our solar system has eight planets, but it's also home to five dwarf planets. Eris, Haumea, Makemake, Ceres and Pluto are all classed as dwarf planets because they don't dictate the orbits of objects in their close vicinity.

Unmanned spaceships, sometimes known as probes, have visited every planet in our solar system. The first probe to visit any planet beyond Earth flew past Venus in 1962, while further afield, *Cassini* orbited Saturn for over a decade.

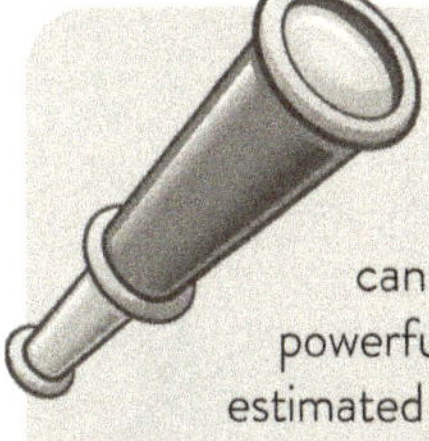

In the observable universe – that's all of the universe that humans can see with their most powerful equipment – there are estimated to be two trillion galaxies! It's worth noting that every galaxy can have millions of stars and there are still parts of the universe we can't see yet!

Though it's always growing, the Sun is already pretty huge. It's estimated that a million Earths could fit into the space that the Sun occupies!

The lower gravity on the Moon has a surprising effect on astronauts. When they're on the satellite, the disks of their spine stretch under the reduced pressure, which can make them up to 5 centimetres taller.

The footprints of the first man on the Moon are still there today. There's no atmosphere on the Moon, so there's no wind to blow them away, which means they're still there today and will be for millions of years, unless someone sweeps over them!

A mechanical phenomenon known as 'cold welding' occurs in space when two metals touch. Because there's no air or atmosphere around the pieces of metal, the molecules don't know that they're separate pieces and join together, without needing to be melted like they would on Earth.

From Earth, we can spot six different galaxies, as well as our own Milky Way. The closest one is Andromeda, but we can also see the Triangulum, Omega Centauri and the Sagittarius Dwarf Spheroidal Galaxy, as well as both Magellanic Clouds.

You might be able to see a giant red spot on images of Jupiter – it's a giant storm that's been raging for years, but it's shrinking! When it was first observed in the 17th century, it was the size of three Earths, but now it's only the size of one.

The largest object that humans have sent to space is the International Space Station. It's 109 metres long and travels around the Earth once every 90 minutes at speeds of over 27,000 kilometres an hour.

Scientists have observed that our galaxy, the Milky Way, is spiral-shaped, but it wasn't the first one we observed. That honour belongs to the Whirlpool Galaxy, sometimes called M51. The M stands for Messier, as the first person to spot it was Charles Messier, way back in 1773.

The rain on Venus isn't made of water like on Earth – it's molten metals. The temperature on Venus is so hot that it can boil metals, turning them into gases, which then cool as they get higher up in the atmosphere and fall as scorching hot liquids.

Neptune was discovered in 1846 and is the furthest planet from the Sun in our solar system. As such, it takes 165 Earth years – or 60,190 days to be exact – for it to complete one orbit of the star. It has only orbited the Sun once since we've known about it!

The first person in space was a Russian called Yuri Gagarin. He reached space on 21 April 1961, beating the American Alan Shepard, who arrived on 5 May in the same year, by two weeks!

The estimated size of the Milky Way galaxy is 107,500 light-years, meaning it would take something travelling at the speed of light over 100,000 years to reach one end from another. With our current technology, it would take us 450 million years to travel across that distance.

The same side of the Moon is always facing Earth! We've never seen the 'dark side of the Moon' because the moon spins at precisely the same speed as it orbits the planet, which is a phenomenon called tidal locking, or synchronous rotation.

Not all unknown territory is out there in the big, wide world: some is inside our own bodies. Microbots are minuscule vehicles that are being developed to enter the human bloodstream and travel around, collecting information and doing little jobs. Hiro uses something similar to microbots in *Big Hero 6*.

In 2014, a man named Les Baugh, who had lost both his arms in an accident, was the first person in history to control prosthetic arms with just his mind. He had surgery to connect his existing nerves to the prosthetics so they could receive messages from the brain.

The word robot has its roots in the Czech word robota, which means forced labour. It formerly referred to lower members of society that did jobs for the rich, but now means anything man-made that can act automatically.

Leonardo da Vinci, who lived in the 15th and 16th centuries, was the first person to sketch out plans for what we think of as a robot. He called it a mechanical knight and it would be able to do simple actions using a pulley. A NASA robotics expert was able to build the knight in 2002 with a few modern adjustments!

Deep Blue was a chess-playing computer that looked at all possible moves and calculated their possible results. Deep Blue could analyse 200 million positions per second. In 1997, it beat the world champion chess player, Garry Kasparov, in a six-game match.

The author Isaac Asimov came up with three laws of robotics in a short story called 'Runaround'. The first law is that robots can't harm humans, the second says that they must obey humans and the final one says they must protect themselves, as long as that doesn't contradict the first two laws!

The first modern robot was built in 1961 by a company called Unimation, started by Joseph Engelberger and George Devol. The robot was called Unimate and was created to help companies like Ford weld together car parts in industrial plants.

Robots can even help us with housework. Robot vacuum cleaners roam around the house, sucking up dirt before returning to its base to be emptied. They have obstacle sensors to avoid things lying around on the ground and 'cliff sensors' to stop them from falling down steep areas like stairs!

Japan has an ageing population, so it's no surprise their government is investing heavily in robots that can take care of them. One of them is called Robear, described as a 'strong robot with a gentle touch'. It's smart and strong enough to be able to lift a human from the ground. Sounds like Baymax from *Big Hero 6*!

South Korea currently has the highest concentration of robots compared to other countries. It has over 900 robots per 10,000 employed people, which is over three times higher than the rates in Europe and the USA.

The US military has been testing out a robot for use in combat. It's a dog-shaped robot that can assist soldiers in battle by carrying resources across terrain effortlessly. It's being developed by a company called Boston Dynamics, which makes several super-advanced robots.

Machines that learn are said to have artificial intelligence, or AI. This means that the machine can sense its environment and respond in ways that make the most sense at that moment. The reason it's called 'artificial intelligence' is because these machines are just collecting data. Whether an action fails or succeeds, the machine records it and over time, it 'learns' the best way to do tasks.

One factory in Japan, owned by a company called FANUC, can operate without a human being present for up to 30 days. It's been operating this way since 2001 and guess what FANUC produce? That's right: robots!

Robots might one day walk among us as equals – in fact the first one already is! A robot called Sophia was granted citizen status by Saudi Arabia in 2017, making her the first robot to be legally recognised as a person in any country.

There's a robot called Raptor that can already run faster than the fastest humans! The Korea Advanced Institute of Science and Technology was inspired by the movements of velociraptors and were able to make Raptor run at a speed of 46 kilometres an hour.

A cyborg is a human that has robotic upgrades, but there aren't many around yet. Cybernetics expert Kevin Warwick may well be the first though. He has computer chips in his arm that let him open doors, control a wheelchair and manoeuvre a prosthetic hand.

A Japanese juice company developed a bizarre robot to help runners stay refreshed. It's called Tomatan and sits on your shoulders while you run, but it isn't just getting a lazy ride – now and then it will offer you a tomato to eat and stop you from running out of energy!

The first robot that was able to look at its surroundings and make decisions for itself was called Shakey. It was created in 1966 at SRI International's Artificial Intelligence Center. It was able to plan, map out routes and perform simple movement tasks.

Robot fights seen in films and TV might be closer to becoming reality than we think. The US company MegaBots challenged Japan's Suidobashi Heavy Industry to a giant robot fight. The Japanese company accepted and in 2017, MegaBots' Eagle One and Suidobashi's Kuratas fought two rounds, winning one apiece.

One of the world's most advanced robots is Atlas, which was created by Boston Dynamics. It's a humanoid robot that can run, jump, hop, flip and interact with its environment. It measures 1.5 metres tall and only weighs 89 kilograms, which isn't much heavier than the average human male.

Robots have already made some jobs redundant and tasks around the farm might be off our to-do list soon too. Farmers currently use robots and drones to dig out weeds, till the land so it's ready for planting, and even help to harvest crops!

To make sure its mobile phones are strong enough to withstand use from humans, Samsung employ a bum-shaped robot to sit on the phone! It's designed to simulate how people normally hold and use their phones – it even wears jeans!

The first robot was created thousands of years ago by a man named Archytas around 400 BC. He created a wooden bird with a steam-powered engine that could fly on its own! It's a far cry from the metal humanoids we think of today, but still, technically, a robot.

At Expo 2010 in Shanghai, China, Toyota demonstrated the precise skills of their Partner Robot by having it play a violin! They hope that one day the robot's precision will be useful for taking care of people with a gentle hand.

When lightning strikes, it creates ozone, which is the chemical that makes up the ozone layer and protects us from UV rays. The lightning splits oxygen into individual molecules, to create 'radicals' or individual oxygen molecules, which then re-form into ozone.

To ignite a fire, you usually need a match or a spark, but fires can start on their own if things get hot enough. This is called spontaneous combustion. It is most common in hay piles and compost heaps, and occurs when chemical reactions create trapped heat. When the heat reaches a certain point, WOOSH! Fire erupts!

Old-fashioned batteries – like the ones labelled AA, AAA, C and D – are full of a chemical called electrolyte and have a terminal on each end. One terminal, called the anode, likes to give out negatively charged particles called electrons. The other terminal, the cathode, likes to receive them. When the terminals are connected, the electrolyte releases electrons, which flow from one terminal to another in an electrical current.

Flames are caused by chemical reactions that give off light and heat at varying levels. Wood fires and candles burn at about 1,093°C. Other substances, such as some oils, waxes and alcohols, burn at less than 149°C.

A gas called nitrogen turns into liquid below –195.79°C. Liquid nitrogen freezes living cells on contact. It is often used to quick-freeze foods. Doctors also use it to freeze moles and other blemishes off people's skin.

Thanks to the strange way its molecules are arranged, water is one of the only substances that expands when it freezes. Most substances shrink when cold, but the molecules in water have a lot of space for bonds to form, which makes ice expand.

You might think graphite, the bit in a pencil that makes the mark on paper, and diamonds used in jewellery couldn't be further apart, but they're both made entirely out of carbon! The only difference is the way that they're formed – diamonds only form under high pressure.

There are only three elements that are liquid at room temperature: mercury, caesium and bromine. A fourth, gallium, is usually a solid, but it will turn into a liquid if it reaches body temperature, for instance, if you had it in the palm of your hand.

Caesium, gold and copper are the only metallic elements that don't appear to be silver. This is because most metals evenly reflect all of the sun's rays, but these three absorb the blue and violet rays, leaving just the yellow and red ones visible.

Every single atom of hydrogen that exists in the universe was created in the Big Bang, 13.8 billion years ago! Other elements were synthesised from these hydrogen atoms, but no new hydrogen atoms have been introduced to the universe.

Astatine is the rarest natural element on the planet, with some estimates suggesting only 25 grams exist in the Earth's crust. If it's needed, which it rarely is, scientists will make it themselves, but only a few micrograms have ever been created.

It, possibly, takes less time for hot water to freeze than it does cold water, which is known as the Mpemba effect. It's named after a Tanzanian teenager who discovered the phenomenon in 1969, but scientists are still arguing about exactly whether it's correct today.

Your stomach is full of acids just as potent as battery acid – if the acids in your stomach were dropped onto your skin, they'd burn through! Luckily the stomach is excellent at keeping the acid in and it's super effective at breaking down the food you eat.

You can't taste salt and that's due to your saliva. As soon as the salt – also known as sodium chloride – touches your spit, it breaks salt down into its components sodium and chlorine. What you actually taste are those two separate elements.

Some elements glow in the dark! Radium is a radioactive material that is commonly shown to glow green, while actinium emanates blue light. Radon, which is normally a gas, will shine with a bright red light if you can cool it down into a solid.

As well as being a useful metal, copper has antibacterial properties! Bacteria dies more quickly on copper than most other materials, including common plastic. In ancient societies, it was used to stop infections from spreading and to lessen pain.

Every element was discovered existing on Earth except helium, which was first discovered by Pierre Jules César Janssen in 1868. He was looking at the sun through an invention called a spectroscope when he observed unusual behaviour caused by helium... the first known record of the element.

The different colours you see when fireworks explode are created using different elements. Magnesium burns white, iron produces yellow, while lithium salts make red sparks. Every firework is packed with different kinds of chemicals for different effects.

A snowflake begins life high in a cold sky, when water vapour freezes around a dust or pollen particle. The icy particle falls downward. More water vapour freezes onto the particle as it falls, forming feathery arms. The conditions are always a little different, so no two snowflakes are alike.

Glass isn't technically a solid. It's another strange state of matter called an amorphous solid, which means it's between a liquid and a solid. The molecules of glass are moving, but they flow so slowly that the glass remains a constant shape.

Helium is the second most common element in the universe, but, because it is lighter than air, it normally floats out of our atmosphere and is very rare on Earth. We can still get our hands on it by mining, as some is trapped underground.

Ethylene is a gas that's naturally created by plants and fruits alike. It's a hormone that encourages plants to mature and fruits to ripen, which is why fruits that produce a lot of ethylene – apples and bananas – can cause other fruits to over-ripen and go off quickly.

Of all the elements in the periodic table, helium is the only one that can't be frozen in the normally occurring atmosphere of our planet. You would need to put helium under a pressure more than 20 times what we have on Earth before it would freeze!

The softest material that naturally occurs in the world is talc – yes, the same talc in talcum powder! It's scientifically known as a hydrated magnesium silicate and it ranks lowest on the Mohs scale that determines hardness – diamonds are at the opposite end of course!

Fear is a reaction to danger. It is part emotional and part physical and stems from a part of the brain called the amygdala. When things happen that could be scary, the amygdala pumps out chemicals that alert the person that something important is going on. Then the person may become afraid. If the amygdala is damaged and does not make these chemicals, a person is less likely to feel fear.

Goosebumps occur when the micro muscles around your hairs contract, which makes the tiny hairs stand up. They normally appear when we're frightened or cold, similar to other mammals, which bristle their hair when they feel threatened.

When human babies are born, their skeletons are not fully formed. Some parts are made of rubbery stuff called cartilage instead of bone. Much of this cartilage is found in the joints, which makes babies very bendy. As babies grow, the cartilage turns into bone, so they become less flexible.

Real people sometimes have bursts of super-strength during emergencies. There are many cases of people lifting cars off accident victims. Scientists think that under stress, our bodies can be flooded with a strength-boosting hormone called adrenaline that allows people to perform superhuman feats.

If you laid the blood vessels of an adult out in a long line, they'd be long enough to wrap around the widest point of Earth more than four times!

Look closely at the palm of your hand and you'll see lots of lines and wrinkles. Everyone has them, and the pattern is different for every person. Palm print identification scans these lines, along with tiny ridges on your skin and compares the scanned image to a stored picture. If the images match, the ID is confirmed, which is a technology used on modern mobile phones.

Synaesthesia is a rare condition where unrelated sensory information gets linked in the brain. People with this condition might hear or taste colours, see smells, or feel an 'eyeball touch' when someone looks at them.

For a long time, lots of people thought the human appendix was a useless organ that we no longer needed. However, scientists now believe that bacteria used in your digestive system go to the appendix to take a break from their hard work!

Humans shed their skin just like a snake does, except we do it little by little. We shed around 30,000 skin cells a minute, and on average our skin is replaced once every month – so you'll have hundreds of different skins during your lifetime!

Your body has three different types of muscles. The smooth muscles (muscles found in your organs) and the cardiac muscle (your heart) work automatically. You can control the third type though – the skeletal muscles. There are about 650 skeletal muscles in your body that make you move.

An amoeba is a one-celled life form that can take many different shapes. It moves by sending out a shoot called a pseudopod, which means 'false foot'. The pseudopod acts sort of like a tunnel, through which the rest of the amoeba flows to a new location.

Humans have more than just five senses. Of course we can see, hear, touch, taste and smell, but we have lots of other ones too. For instance, you can feel the heat from the Sun on a warm day, but you're not touching it. We have lots of secret senses like that beyond the basic five!

Have you ever seen the little bumps on your tongue? Many people think those are the tastebuds, but they're actually the papillae. Tastebuds are invisible to our eyesight, but they do sit on top of those papillae lumps!

An adult or teenager's eyes blink on average 21,000 times in a single day, or more than 900 times an hour! The muscle that controls blinking is the fastest in the human body, able to contract in less than a hundredth of a second!

You don't have any muscles in your fingers. Your fingers move thanks to tendons, which are controlled by the muscles in your forearm. Over 33 percent of your hand's strength comes from the tendons in your little finger!

Your skin varies in thickness depending on what part of the body it's covering. It's thickest on your feet, where it measures 1.4 millimetres, but on your eyelids, where the skin is thinnest, it's just 0.2 millimetres!

The largest organ in our body is the liver and it also has incredible regeneration skills. If just a quarter of the liver remains, it will still be able to completely recover to a full organ, unless it's damaged or scarred.

The nails on your fingers grow twice as fast as your toenails – so you need to trim them twice as often! The nail on your little finger will grow the slowest out of all your digits and the big toenail grows fastest on your feet.

If, like the average person, you spend two minutes brushing your teeth in the morning and again before you go to bed, you'll spend over 70 days of your life keeping your teeth clean. And that doesn't even include flossing time!

The transparent front of your eye, called the cornea, is the only part of your body that doesn't receive oxygen from your blood. Instead, as it's exposed directly to the atmosphere, it gets its oxygen straight from the air in front of it.

Have you ever wondered why your belly makes noises? It's normally just the sound of your digestive system working its way through the food you've eaten, but it can sometimes be gas or a sign it can't digest certain foods. There's even a special word for the noises your belly makes: borborygmi!

A growth of cells is known as a tumour, which can often cause illnesses and death, although they're becoming less fatal as scientists discover how to treat them. One type of tumour, called a teratoma, can even grow its own hair, muscles and bones.

The beating sound of a heart is an opening and shutting rather than the bang of a drum. Every beat you hear is one of the heart's valves opening to let blood pump through then slamming shut again.

Your bum is the biggest muscle in your body. It's scientific name is the gluteus maximus, or glute for short, and you have two of them – one in each bum cheek! They form the main muscle that controls the movement of your hips.

A newborn baby's eyes are two-thirds the size that they'll be when they reach adulthood. Considering the difference in size between an adult and a baby, that's huge! Your nose and your ears, on the other hand, will never stop growing!

Your body is made up of trillions of cells, but did you know that they're not all human? In fact, there are ten times more bacteria cells in your body than there are human ones. But there's nothing to worry about – they're all helpful and we need them to survive!

The rarest eye colour you can have is green – only 2 percent of people in the world have green eyes. Babies are always born with blue or brown eyes as it can take up to three years for green eyes to develop.

Static electricity can form an invisible field that makes your hair stand on end. Rub a balloon against your hair to see and feel it for yourself! This type of electricity can also zap you, like when you touch a doorknob after walking across a carpeted surface. A spark snaps against your finger as the electricity discharges.

Sneezes feel like powerful forces sometimes, especially when they happen suddenly, and there's a good reason why: the average sneeze is expelled at over 160 km/h. That's faster than a car is allowed to travel on most roads!

Water is made up of hydrogen and oxygen, which form water molecules. Water molecules are strongly attracted to each other, but not as strongly attracted to air. This means that wherever water meets air, the water molecules cling together extra tightly. This is called surface tension.

A force called gravity pulls a falling person downward. When a parachute's fabric spreads out and pushes against the air, this force is called air resistance. The air resistance works against gravity and slows the person wearing a parachute to a safe speed.

Magnets have two poles. Scientists call them north and south. Opposite poles attract each other, but similar poles push against or repel each other. Try to shove two like poles together, and you'll see for yourself: an invisible force field makes it impossible!

The femur, the bone in the top of your leg that joins your hip to your knee, is the longest bone in your body. It accounts for around a quarter of your height.

Our planet has its very own force field! Earth is surrounded by an invisible magnetic field. This field blocks many particles streaming from the Sun and sends them back into space. That's lucky for us, because too many of the Sun's particles would hurt living plants and animals – including people!

It's impossible to breathe and swallow at the same time because of a flap of tissue called the epiglottis, which blocks food from your airways. Scientists think that this is an evolutionary trait that stops humans from choking on food that they're eating, or even their own saliva.

Three of the most well-known phases of matter are solid, liquid and gas. Water has each of these three phases. Water's gas phase is called vapour, which is invisible. Sometimes, though, water vapour forms tiny liquid drops that are too light to fall out of the air. These drops can collect into steam and clouds, which we can see.

Scientists believe there are still many mysterious, undiscovered forms of energy in the universe. Zero-point energy is one of them. If it does exist, it would come from subatomic particles, smaller than atoms. These particles would never be completely still and scientists think they constantly flicker from one state to another. This activity might make energy that could be collected.

There are more than twenty different states of matter. The three main states are solid, liquid and gas. Lightning and ionised neon in signs are examples of a fourth – plasma – but then they start to get really weird. For instance, one state of matter is superfluid, which is a liquid that can flow without friction.

An oobleck is a strange substance that shifts between phases of matter. When left alone, it is generally a runny liquid, but if you apply force to it in any way – such as hitting or pulling it – the oobleck becomes a hard solid. A mixture of water and cornstarch is an example of an oobleck.

Isaac Newton developed his three laws of motion after an apple fell on his head while he was sitting under a tree. His laws changed the way that we looked at forces applied on objects and how they affect movement.

Our fingers are electric! When you press the screen of a smartphone, your touch is registered because a small amount of electricity passes through the skin on your fingers – which is why it doesn't work through gloves for instance.

You're made up of trillions of atoms, but you're still 99.9 percent empty space! Atoms normally contain a nucleus and electrons, but if the atom was the size of a cathedral, the nucleus would be the size of your fist, and the electron the size of a moth!

We've been able to observe just five percent of the universe. How do we know this if we don't know what's there? Scientists can see the effects of energy that they can't account for in the known universe and have calculated that we can't see all the mass that should be there, which has led to the theory that dark matter and dark energy fill up the remaining 95 percent!

Water can freeze and boil at the same temperature. To reach this 'triple point', where it can exist as all three main states of matter, water needs to be put under a certain amount of pressure: a lot higher than we normally have on Earth.

When a toy car loops the loop, why doesn't it fall? At the top of the loop, gravity is pulling the car downward. But at the same time, the car's forward motion around a curved loop creates something called a centrifugal force, which keeps the car and track against each other. The greater the speed, the greater the centrifugal force. If the centrifugal force is stronger than gravity, the car doesn't fall.

Light travels at around 300,000 kilometres a second when travelling through a vacuum such as space. However, it can be slowed down. In water, it travels at three-quarters of that speed and the slowest light has been recorded at just 61 km/h.

Which falls faster: a ton of feathers or a ton of bricks? Well, gravity pulls all things to the ground equally, so they'll both hit the ground at the same time in a vacuum! A single feather normally falls more slowly because it is subject to another great force present in Earth's atmosphere: air resistance.

The Large Hadron Collider is a particle accelerator that can speed up particles to just under the speed of light. But that's just the start. Scientists smash these particles together to create new particles and the collision, for a fraction of a nanosecond, is hotter than the Sun!

Friction is a force that acts against a moving object, generating heat as it slows an object, which is why you'll sometimes get a burn going down a slide. Water and ice reduce friction, which is why water slides are less likely to burn you, and you slip and slide around on ice.

Astronauts can't burp in space and it's all gravity's fault! Normally when you eat food, the solids and liquids used in digestion sink due to gravity, while gases stay at the top of your digestive system to be pumped out of your oesophagus. But in space, where there's no gravity, the solids and liquids stay mixed with the gases!

Archimedes made a scientific discovery in the bath. When he sat in it, he realised that the amount of water displaced by him getting into the bath was equal to his weight – the water has a 'buoyancy' force that acts against gravity and is now used to determine the density of materials. Eureka!

If you spin a ball while you drop it from a great height, it will travel down due to gravity, but also sideways! The spin of the ball pulls some of the air with it, which makes it travel along an unusual path. This phenomenon is known as the Magnus effect.

To make porcelain, Chinese artists of the Han dynasty heated clay and other materials to a high temperature. The process resulted in a strong material useful for making pottery, sculptures and decorations. Some artists would paint patterns and pictures on the porcelain before heating it, which turned it into enamel.

You can feel friction in the air, which is sometimes known as 'drag'. If you jump out of a plane, your body is pulled by gravity and as you accelerate, you'll feel the drag in the opposite direction like a strong wind. When these two forces balance, it's called the terminal velocity – the fastest speed an object can fall.

A device called the aqualung lets people explore under the sea. Invented in 1943 by oceanographers Jacques-Yves Cousteau and Émile Gagnan, it was the first practical **s**elf-**c**ontained **u**nderwater **b**reathing **a**pparatus, or SCUBA. Scuba equipment lets people carry their own air supply underwater for adventures.

Besides compasses, historical explorers used other navigation tools like sextants that measure the relative position of stars and planets in the sky and chronometers, which are super-precise timekeepers. Used together, these measurements helped explorers determine where they were on Earth.

Long-ago cartographers (map makers) had to do their best to draw images of what they found, but the resulting maps were not very accurate. Nowadays satellites circle our planet, taking pictures of everything below. We know exactly what most of Earth's surface looks like and how most of its landmasses are shaped.

A compass is a tool which contains a magnetised metal that aligns with Earth's magnetic north pole and is used in navigation. Compasses were invented during the Han dynasty, around 200 BC and they were made from a plate with a spoon carved from lodestone. Compasses weren't used outside of China until over a thousand years later, in AD 1190.

Clouds look like light, fluffy objects, but they could weigh somewhere in the region of 500,000 kilograms! The water in clouds is spread so thinly and the droplets are so small that the air resistance is greater than gravity and the cloud floats!

The Chinese system of writing has been in use for over 3,500 years. The Chinese language uses symbols called characters. Chinese is written in columns, so you read characters from top to bottom and columns from right to left. The language includes thousands of characters that people memorise.

A Han dynasty astronomer named Zhang Heng invented the first earthquake detector. The device showed which direction an earthquake was coming from. It could detect an earthquake from over 1,000 kilometres away.

Aztec, Olmec and Maya people built large stone calendars to keep time by tracking the movements of the Sun, planets and stars. The Aztecs carved a calendar out of basalt, a volcanic rock, which is now on display at the National Museum of Anthropology in Mexico City.

Firecrackers were invented early in China's Han dynasty, when they discovered that setting bamboo on fire exploded with a loud sound. When the Chinese created gunpowder during the Tang dynasty, the first fireworks were made by putting gunpowder into bamboo stalks and throwing them on a fire. Over the next centuries, the Chinese developed the technology to fire explosives into the air and used weapons like the rocket cannon in battle.

In Southeast Asia, monks used palm-leaf manuscripts to spread information. These manuscripts were made from small rectangular sections of dried palm leaves. They contain early poetry, art, philosophy and stories. Some manuscripts are over 1,000 years old!

Pictures became an important way to share knowledge for societies that historically didn't have a written language, such as the Hmong from the highlands of mainland Southeast Asia. Hmong women incorporated pictures and patterns in embroidered quilts that told the stories of their people.

Prostheses are mechanical parts that replace limbs or other human body parts. The first known prosthetic was a wooden toe from Ancient Egypt, but the first moving prosthetics were fashioned in the 1500s by a French surgeon called Ambroise Paré. He utilised locks and harnesses to recreate limb movement.

People can wear wingsuits, which have flaps of parachute fabric between the arms and legs to let them glide. Wearing the suit, a person leaps off a cliff or out of a plane, then spreads their arms and legs into an 'X' position. The wingsuit creates air resistance and lets the person soar!

Hydroflyers work like rockets, but they use water instead of hot gases. A person straps their feet into the board's built-in boots and a hose delivers water to the device. This water blasts from nozzles on the bottom of the board with a force hard enough to lift the user 15 metres into the air!

Scientists use telescopes to get a closer look at objects in the sky. Telescopes are tools that make distant objects appear bigger and clearer. In the last 200 years, telescopes have gotten much more powerful and we even have telescopes in space.

Scientists are working to develop programmable matter. This is any substance that can be changed or controlled by people, like for instance, a gel that might turn hard when electricity is applied. Robots or other materials might be programmed to form tools with different purposes. There could be a single tool that could change in an instant from a wire cutter to a screwdriver to a knife.

GPS stands for Global Positioning System, which is a network consisting of a minimum of 24 Earth-orbiting satellites. At least four of the satellites are visible from any point on Earth at any moment, so that a GPS receiver on Earth can measure the distance to all visible satellites and use this information to calculate its own position.

Toy designers today can use three-dimensional (3-D) printers to create sample toys and parts. A 3-D printer works by building up objects in layers. Each layer is printed using plastic or another material and when it dries, another layer is added on top. This process is repeated many times to create a three-dimensional object.

It's amazing how many inventions were created mistakenly. The tea bag was another happy accident, created when Thomas Sullivan decided to send samples of tea he was selling in silk bags. Potential customers thought they were meant to be dunked in hot water and the tea bag was born!

The original voice actor for Tigger from the film *Winnie the Pooh* was a man called Paul Winchell. Not only was he a splendiferous voice artist, but he was also the first person to build and patent a working artificial mechanical heart.

Bubble wrap – the poppy plastic packaging material – is a failed invention! Its creators Alfred Fielding and Marc Shuvon were instead trying to create a three-dimensional wallpaper out of plastic.

You're never too young to be an inventor. Braille was invented by a 15-year-old boy called Louis Braille, who made an alphabet of raised dots for blind people to read. Before that, blind people had to trace over raised letters, which was much harder.

It is thought that Alfred Nobel started the Nobel Prize because a newspaper accidentally ran a story about his death and he didn't like the title. Because he invented dynamite, the newspaper called him 'the merchant of death', so it is believed he made the Nobel Prize to reward discoveries and associate his name with something nicer!

The car manufacturer Volvo created the three-point seatbelt that most cars use today. Instead of patenting their safety feature and making money from it, they freely allowed other car-makers to use it in their vehicles so that they could all be as safe.

Velcro was created by a man named George de Mestral, who noticed that burs – a type of seed that some plants have – were sticking to his socks and his dog's fur. He looked at the burs under a microscope and discovered they were covered in hooks, which he copied to make Velcro!

The most famous accidental discovery is by a Scottish scientist named Alexander Fleming. He left a petri dish of bacteria uncovered while he went away and discovered a mould had formed that killed a lot of the bacteria. This mould was the basis of penicillin, which is used in medicine today and has saved millions of lives.

When the Wright brothers finally perfected the flying machine, its first flight lasted just 12 seconds and travelled 36 metres. That's shorter than the wingspan of a Boeing 747 that most airlines operate today!

The invention of the steam engine changed the course of history. Steam engines had been around in the 17th century, but James Watt created a new type in 1765 that used a more efficient circular motion and ended up being used in mills, canals and trains over the next two centuries.

If you're reading this as a printed book, then thank Johannes Gutenberg. He was a German inventor who created the printing press, which allowed books and other literature to be printed repeatedly. Before then, any piece of writing was usually done by hand!

Marie Curie was a trailblazing inventor, who used her discovery of the elements radium and polonium to create X-rays that can see through our skin! She won two Nobel Prizes for her work, but unfortunately died of radiation exposure from the highly radioactive radium and polonium.

Bessie Coleman was the first woman of African-American and Native American descent to hold a pilot's license. She earned the licence in 1921 but sadly died in 1926, when she crashed while testing a new aeroplane. This bold explorer paved the way for many others to follow.

An engine that uses gas has a special name: an internal combustion engine, which means fuels are burned inside the engine. Fuel is pumped into the engine and a tiny electrical spark sets off an explosion, which causes a force strong enough to make the pistons within the engine to turn. The engine causes the crankshaft to turn, and that's what makes the wheels turn.

Rockets are full of fuel, which, when ignited, causes gases to blast downward out of a hole and the force pushes the rocket upward. A rocket must travel about 40,000 km/h to escape Earth's gravity and reach orbit. That's 11.3 km/s!

Drones use whirling wings called propellers to create thrust. The speed of the propellers controls the amount of thrust, and when the propellers spin very quickly, the thrust is greater than gravity, causing the drone to rise. When the drone reaches the desired height, the operator slows the propellers until thrust and gravity are equal and the drone hovers in place.

Stealth planes are nearly invisible to radar. When these waves hit a regular plane, they bounce back and the radar gets the echoes and 'sees' the object. Stealth planes have a special shape, colour and paint that scatter most of the waves instead of echoing them back.

No matter how fast you drive, you'll never be able to go as fast as the airbags built into your vehicle. They can take just 40 milliseconds to shoot out at a speed of 7,200 km/h before inflating to protect you from banging your head!

The 24 Hours of Le Mans is an endurance race in France that lets drivers test how well cars hold up after 24 hours of high-speed driving. The race takes place on a circuit of nearly 137 kilometres that includes both a curvy track and closed streets. Pit stops in this race, where tyres are changed and fuel tanks are filled, are as important as the driving. Sometimes repairs are made and drivers jump out and make way for their driving partners.

Car makers are testing driverless cars right now! These cars have cameras, lasers, radar and special sensors to show them where to steer. They will be able to 'talk' to each other, so they stay out of each other's way too.

NASCAR races feature cars like Bobby Swift from *Cars 3*. The most famous race is the Daytona 500 in Florida, USA. Roughly 50 cars do 200 laps around the 4-kilometre track. Even though these cars are reaching speeds of over 300 km/h, it's okay for them to have 'contact', which is a nice way of saying that they can try to push each other out of the way!

Tuk-tuks are open-air rickshaw taxis, known more for their style and sputtering than their top speeds, but are great at weaving through traffic.

Traditional wooden boats, sometimes known as longtails, are the Southeast Asian tuk-tuks of the rivers and sea. Perfected over the centuries, these boats were designed with high fronts and flat bottoms that allow them to easily glide through rough waves, shallow water and narrow passages.

The world's deepest diving sub is called the *Limiting Factor*. In May 2019, Victor Vescovo piloted this vessel to a depth of 10,928 metres, which was 16 metres deeper than any previous dive by humans. At that depth, the pressure on the vessel was more than 177 times greater than the pressure at sea level!

The Ford Model T was the first car mass-produced for the public and was first made in 1908. With the introduction of the assembly line method of manufacturing, Henry Ford managed to reduce the amount of time it took to build a Model T from one every 12 hours to one every three minutes!

Leonardo da Vinci sketched out a plan for something resembling a car in 1478! The car was recently built and is on display in Florence's Institute and Museum of the History of Science.

The world's first practical fuel-powered car was invented in 1885 by Carl Benz, who would go on to create the Mercedes-Benz car manufacturer. It was called the Benz Patent Motorwagen and could reach a top speed of just 16 km/h!

There's a fleet of 14 super police cars in Dubai that contains a Bugatti Veyron among its vehicles. It's the world's fastest police car and one of the fastest cars in the world, able to reach speeds of up to 407 km/h.

Maglevs are super speedy trains that use magnetic levitation – which is where it gets its name from – to reduce friction and travel over 400 km/h! It doesn't have any wheels following a track, which is where friction usually comes from, but uses magnets to lift and power it forward over a central path.

The land speed record is held by a vehicle called the *ThrustSSC*, which reached a whopping 1,228 km/h! It achieved the feat in 1997 on the super-flat surface of North America's Black Rock Desert.

The longest journey you can complete by train begins in Porto, Portugal and arrives in Singapore, which takes at least 12 whole days. It's a 16,000 kilometre journey that takes you from the westernmost point of Europe to South Asia, although you have to change trains along the way!

The longest car in the world is a limousine created by Jay Ohrberg in California. It's 30 metres long and has its own swimming pool and helipad. However, it must be a nightmare turning corners in such a long vehicle!

The two coasts of Australia weren't joined by railway until 1970. The *Indian Pacific* travels between Perth in the west and Sydney in the east, it travels along the longest straight railway (478 kilometres) and its only schedule stop is at Cook railway station!

The Seiryu Miharashi train station in Japan can only be reached by train. Passengers can alight to a small viewing platform while the train makes a ten-minute stop, but it only serves as a sightseeing spot for the Nishiki River.

The USA has the longest railway network by distance covered. It spans over 250,000 kilometres and is more than twice as big as China's, which is the next largest. About 80 percent of it is used primarily for freight trains.

When Abraham Lincoln was assassinated in 1865, his body was transported to his home state of Illinois by train, passing through 180 cities. This meandering journey helped popularise the use of train travel in the USA.

The first recognised steam train was based on Robert Stephenson's 'Rocket'. It competed against four other steam locomotives in 1829 so that the Liverpool and Manchester Railway could choose which one would pull their trains.

San Marino is the only nation in the world that has more cars than people. For every adult, there's an average of 1.6 registered cars. Compare that to the US which has 0.87 cars per person.

The world record sailing speed – that's just using wind – is held by Australian Paul Larsen. He reached a speed of 65.45 knots – that's the equivalent of around 121 km/h on land.

The youngest person to sail around the world is Laura Dekker, who cast off in 2010 at the age of just 14 years old. A lengthy 518 days later, aged 16, she finished her journey when she landed in the port of Simpson Bay, Sint Maarten.

Aeroplanes are specifically designed to be able to withstand a lightning strike! It's estimated that on average every single plane in the world is struck once a year, but the plane is engineered to discharge it without any damage.

Some damages to planes can be fixed with sticky tape – although a very special kind. It's called speed tape and is a strong adhesive that contains aluminium, which is strong enough to deal with cosmetic repairs until parts are available to replace them.

The Concorde jet was a plane that flew passengers between London and New York in around three hours – less than half the time it normally takes. It could break the sound barrier (the speed of sound, also known as Mach 1) and actually went twice as fast, reaching a top speed of Mach 2.04!

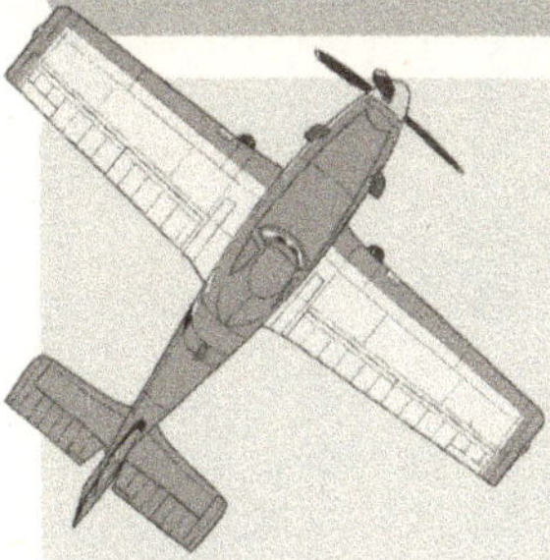

At any point in time, there are something close to 8,000 planes in flight above your head. That's well over a million people flying at once! The United States accounts for more than half of these planes, with up to 5,000 in their airspace at any given moment.

London has had underground trains since 1863. The Metropolitan Line was the first to open up London's underground system, which was also the first one in the world. The steam and smoke created by the trains often filled the tunnel and made journeys quite unpleasant.

The world's biggest dump truck is the BelAZ 75710, which operates at a coal mine in Belarus. Its wheels alone are 4 metres tall! It's as long as two double-decker buses parked end-to-end and can carry up to 450 tonnes at once.

The Netherlands has more bikes per person than any other country in the world. Over 85 percent of over-15s own a bicycle and 30 percent of all journeys are made on two wheels. Pedal power!

The earliest relative of a bicycle was created by Karl Drais in Germany around 1817. He wanted a horseless carriage, but he didn't think to include any pedals to turn the wheels on his invention. Instead, he used his feet to push himself along the ground!

# LEISURE

It's time to sit comfortably, kick up your feet and leisurely browse a collection of facts all about the things you do in your free time. Ever wondered where the sandwich comes from? Or how much pocket money you would need to buy the world's most expensive toy? Find out the answers in these fact-filled pages!

The Chinese invented kites over 2,000 years ago, using bamboo for the frames and silk for the fabric. Flying kites became a popular activity, but did you know that kites were also a useful tool? Written records show that the Chinese used kites to send messages, measure distances and test the wind.

Around 34,000 BC, textiles were developed. Textiles are flexible materials made of a network of fibres, like fabric and cloth. These materials can be cut or torn into the needed shape, then sewn back together with needle and thread. The earliest cloth dolls probably appeared soon after clothing did! Dolly from *Toy Story 3* is a good example of a cloth doll.

Mexicans may invite their friends over to eat some cake on their birthday and sing 'Las Mañanitas', the traditional Mexican birthday song. Some people hang a piñata from a high place, put on a blindfold and spin around. Then they try to hit the piñata with a stick to break it open, and cause the candy or toys inside to spill out.

The company that produces the most tyres isn't a car manufacturer – it's LEGO! They produce an average of around 838,000 rubber wheels every day, not for the cars on the road, but for the vehicles in their sets.

LEGO was invented in 1949 by a Danish man called Ole Kirk Christiansen. He started his business after receiving a plastic moulding machine a few years earlier, which he used to make plastic teddy bears before he designed the classic LEGO brick.

Injection moulding is a process in which molten plastic is injected into a hollow mould, where it cools and hardens within seconds. The finished object is ejected from the mould once it's solid and new plastic is injected. An injection moulding machine can quickly turn out thousands of identical objects – like toy soldiers!

The Slinky, the basis for *Toy Story's* Slinky Dog, was not designed as a toy. It was created by engineer Richard James in 1943 as a spring meant to stabilise instruments on ships in rough seas. It didn't work well for its intended use, so James decided to market it as a toy and one of history's most successful playthings was born.

Many balls were originally made of rubber, which comes from trees! It is harvested mostly in India and Malaysia and starts as a sap called latex. To collect the latex, tubes called taps are inserted into tree trunks and the latex runs out into buckets. It is taken to a factory and processed into dry rubber and used for bouncy balls.

A pull-back vehicle is a variation of a wind-up toy. Instead of winding a knob, a person makes the car's wheels rotate. The toy stores this energy in a mainspring, just like other wind-up toys. As the energy is released, ZOOM! The car zips forward!

Evidence of marbles has been found as far back as Ancient Egypt. Gems crafted into marble-like shapes were found buried alongside an Egyptian child who lived over 5,000 years ago.

The first toy to be advertised on TV was Mr Potato Head! Adverts selling the creative spud pioneered by George Lerner were first aired in 1952 – except it didn't contain the potato, just the accessories. And of course, you might have seen Mr Potato Head in the *Toy Story* films, too...

As if sending rockets into space wasn't fun enough, NASA engineer Dr Lonnie Johnson also created and patented the Super Soaker water pistol and the Nerf Gun. Those are just two of over 250 patents he owns!

It is believed that the first jigsaw puzzle was created by a teacher named John Spilsbury in around 1760. He cut a map into pieces to try to teach his students about the geography of the world, but eventually started cutting other images into pieces too.

The term 'china doll' refers to dolls with shiny porcelain heads and body parts, just like Bo Peep from *Toy Story*. Porcelain is a ceramic made by heating clay that contains a material called kaolin in a kiln to temperatures of about 1,425°C. The technique came from China around 1,200 years ago and slowly spread around the world. Most antique china dolls come from Germany, which had a booming doll industry in the mid-to late-1800s.

Barbie actually has a full name: Barbara Millicent Roberts. She was named after the daughter of the creator, Ruth Handler, while Ken was named after Ruth's son, Kenneth.

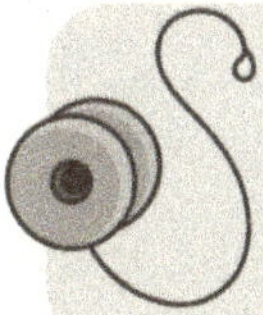

The existence of yo-yos is older than you might think. Archaeologists have discovered one among the artefacts of Ancient Greece during the period of 500 BC, which dates the yo-yo at around 2,500 years old.

The most expensive toy in the world may be a doll's house that sold for $8.5 million back in 2015! The Astolat Dollhouse Castle is an intricate multi-storey doll's house, with 29 rooms, stained glass windows and even a working fireplace.

The wooden nesting doll, or matryoshka, originated in Russia. These dolls were once made and painted entirely by hand. Each set must be made from the same piece of wood, because wood expands and shrinks depending on the amount of moisture in the air, but the same piece of wood will swell and shrink in the same way. If different woods are used, the dolls won't nest correctly.

Minecraft, the blocky building and survival game from Swedish developer Mojang Studios, is one of the best-selling video games of all time. It's sold over 300 million copies. It's only outsold by the timeless classic Tetris, which has sold over 520 million copies, mostly through mobile downloads.

The teddy bear is named after US President Theodore Roosevelt, who often went by the name of Teddy. An inventor created a stuffed toy called Teddy's Bear after hearing that the president refused to shoot a wounded baby bear when he was on a hunt.

In Surrey, England, there was a house made entirely out of LEGO. It was built by a man called James May and had a working shower and toilet too. LEGO liked it so much, they tried to buy it and move it to LEGOLAND in Windsor.

Yo-yos are marvels of energy transfer! A still yo-yo in your hand has potential, or kinetic, energy. As it drops or rises, it has two kinds of kinetic energy: movement up and down, and rotation, because it is spinning on a central rod called an axle. Friction slows the yo-yo down, but you can keep it going by gently yanking the string and adding energy back into the system.

The Frisbee started as a cake pan! Walter Frederick Morrison accidentally invented it in 1937 when he was throwing items around with his wife on the beach. One man offered to buy the cake pan they were chucking between them for 25 cents and the Frisbee was born – though it wouldn't be named that until two decades later.

The Rubik's Cube, created by a Hungarian man named Ernő Rubik has over 43 quintillion possible arrangements, but only one of them will show all the colours separated on different faces. The exact number of arrangements is 43,252,003,274,489,856,000!

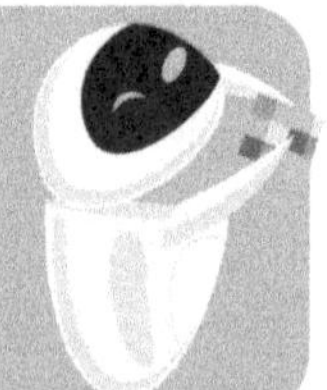

The number of ways that a deck of 52 cards can be arranged is greater than the number of stars in the Milky Way galaxy – by quite a lot! There are 400,000,000,000 – 400 billion – stars in the Milky Way, whereas the number of deck arrangements is 80 unvigintillion – that's an 8 with 66 zeroes after it!

Nintendo, the company that makes the Switch console, was established over 100 years ago in 1889. Back then they made playing cards, but they've also tackled other industries like running hotels and ferrying people in taxis before they made the switch to video games.

During World War II, the British government sent British prisoners of war board games to play. They sent Monopoly sets that had secret maps, real money and tiny tools to help them escape from their prison.

South Korea had a rule called the Cinderella Law, which banned children under the age of 16 from playing video games after midnight and before six in the morning! It was passed into law in 2011 to try and prevent game addiction, but was cancelled in 2021.

Play-Doh was originally used to clean soot off of walls, but with more homes adopting gas and electric heating instead of coal, its creator turned it into a modelling clay and launched it into the toy realm in 1956.

The skateboard was most likely invented in California, USA in the 1940s, when surfers were looking for thrills when the waves weren't rolling in. For this reason, it was sometimes known as 'sidewalk surfing'.

In *Raya and the Last Dragon*, Raya's fighting style is inspired by Arnis, the celebrated national martial arts of the Philippines. Arnis, also known as kali or escrima, uses many different weapons: sticks, knives, blades and other improvised weapons.

One of the most famous styles of kung fu is Shaolin kung fu, named for a monastery located in Henan, China. The Shaolin monks follow a religion called Buddhism and many of the monks learned kung fu to protect their temple. Shaolin kung fu strongly influenced much of the Chinese martial arts we see today.

During Mulan's fight with Shan Yu in the film *Mulan*, the title character uses her fan to twist away his sword. Some forms of Chinese martial arts incorporate the use of fans. Fans designed for fighting were foldable and made of metal or wood and the ends of the fan were sharp, making it a dangerous weapon.

The first Olympic Games were held in the city of Olympia in Ancient Greece in around 776 BC to celebrate the god Zeus. Events included wrestling, chariot racing and javelin and all competitors that took part had to be naked!

Runner Usain Bolt is the fastest human on Earth. In 2011, Bolt reached a top speed of 43.99 km/h in a 100-metre race. For non-athletes, a typical top speed is closer to 24 km/h.

The biggest cycling race in the world is the Tour de France, which takes place every year across the European countryside. The race is split into different segments across 23 or 24 days and hundreds of cyclists cover approximately 3,500 kilometres from start to finish!

Since 1928, every Olympic Games has been accompanied by the Olympic flame, which burns for the duration of the event. The flame is always lit by the sun in Olympia and is passed between torch-bearers across the world before it arrives at the destination city.

Although the first Olympics took place over 2,500 years ago, they were cancelled in the 4th century and didn't start again for 1,500 years! The 'modern' Olympics began in 1896 when it was revived by a Frenchman called Pierre de Coubertin.

In 1923, a jockey named Frank Hayes suffered a heart attack and died while he was riding a horse during a race in Belmont Park, New York. However, the horse carried on and passed the finish line before everyone else, meaning that Frank won his last race.

The arts of fighting and self-defence are called martial arts, though some often use the term kung fu to refer to Chinese martial arts. Kung fu dates back over 2,500 years and originally focused on fighting without weapons. By the Han dynasty, kung fu had evolved to include fighting with swords, wooden poles and spears.

The Dragon Boat Festival takes place in the summer in China. It honours Qu Yuan, a famous poet who was also a government official. Popular traditions include racing boats decorated to look like dragons and eating zongzi – a dumpling made from rice and fillings and wrapped in bamboo leaves.

The gold medals that Olympians win only contain around 6 grams of gold. It's been that way since 1912, when the medals were completely made out of their respective metals – gold, silver and bronze!

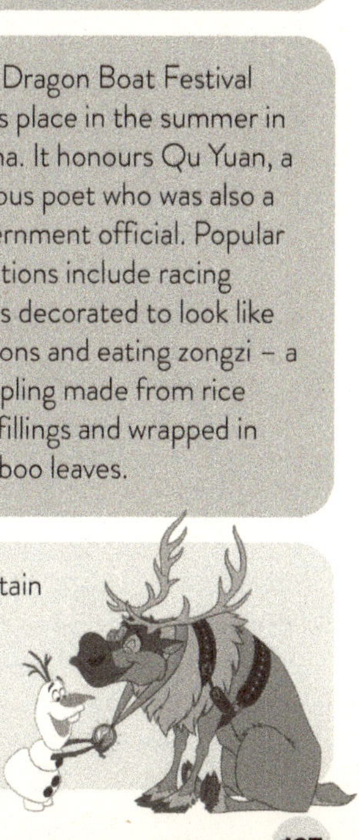

In 2004, Danny 'Shiphtur' Le became the first gamer to receive an athlete's visa to the USA. He competed in eSports playing a game called League of Legends and needed a visa to play for his American team.

Melbourne in Australia hosted the 1956 edition of the Olympic Games, but because its quarantine laws meant that horses couldn't enter for the equestrian events, Stockholm had to host those five months before the rest of the summer games!

Umpires that work in the Major League Baseball franchise have to wear black underwear according to the laws of the game. They crouch and squat a lot, so the rule is supposed to stop them from showing a tear in their trousers if they stretch too far!

Wimbledon hosted the longest tennis match in the world, between John Isner and Nicolas Mahut. It lasted over 11 hours and the final set contained 138 matches alone! Isner eventually won the set by a score of 70–68 and moved on to the next round.

While pitching in the final inning of a match against the Philadelphia Athletics in 1919, Cleveland pitcher Ray Caldwell was struck by lightning. Remarkably, he carried on playing and Cleveland won the match thanks to his pitches!

Lionel Messi holds the record for the most appearances at football's World Cup. His 26th appearance took him past German defender Lothar Matthäus in 2022, the same year that he also lifted the trophy with Argentina for the first time.

Cristiano Ronaldo has two forenames and he was named after the US President Ronald Reagan, who was an actor before becoming president. Ronaldo's father was a fan of his movies and gave his son the full name Cristiano Ronaldo dos Santos Aveiro.

Swimmer Michael Phelps is the most decorated Olympian in history. He competed in five consecutive Olympic Games, beginning with Sydney in 2000, and picked up 28 medals in all competitions, including 23 golds!

Phelps, of the USA, also holds the record for the most medals picked up in a single Olympic games, winning eight in both 2004 and 2008. However, his 2004 haul included two bronzes, while 2008 was all gold medals!

No one knows for certain why tennis is scored in the weird way it is. The best theory is that the numbers followed the quarters on a clockface – 15, 30, 45 – but the 5 in 45 was dropped for some reason. Using love for zero is also thought to be a mistranslation from French, where they might have called the egg-looking number *l'oeuf*!

Volleyballs were originally made from the bladder – the very bouncy inside bit – of a basketball! William G. Morgan, who invented the sport in 1896 wanted to use a basketball, but it was too heavy, so he cut the bladder out and used that instead.

The England women's national football team, known as the Lionesses, became the fifth football team to lift the Women's European Championship trophy in 2022, a year when they went completely unbeaten. They played 20 matches altogether and won all but four of them, which they drew.

Every ball pitched in Major League Baseball is dirty! To make the balls less shiny and easier to grip, the organisation wipes mud over every baseball before it is ready to pitch. This has been done for over 75 years.

Since 1980, Kenyans have dominated men's long-distance races. Most of them, like marathon record-holder Eliud Kipchoge, come from a tribe called the Kalenjin. This group of tribes contains over 6 million people across Kenya and Uganda and is sometimes known as 'the running tribe'.

Wembley Stadium in the United Kingdom is the second biggest football arena in Europe, second only to Barcelona's Camp Nou. It can seat over 90,000 people and has a staggering 2,618 toilets!

The most watched sports event is the FIFA World Cup, where players from 32 countries compete to be crowned the best footballing nation. The 2022 edition was hosted in Qatar in the winter months and was watched by 5.4 billion people!

After the fall of the USSR, Lithuania couldn't afford to go to the 1992 Olympic Games. A US band called The Grateful Dead sponsored the country's basketball team to go, even designing a kit for them to wear, and Lithuania received a bronze medal!

A 100-year-old man named Fauja Singh broke the world records for centenarians – people over the age of 100 – in eight different distances, ranging from the 100-metre sprint to a mile-long run.

Tofu is a type of curd made from mashed soybeans that is pressed into soft white blocks. The earliest record of tofu being made comes from the Han dynasty. Tofu itself doesn't have much flavour, so it can be prepared with soy sauce, ginger, garlic and spices. Tofu can even be served as a sweet dessert!

The first oranges to arrive in the Western world from Southeast Asia were actually green! In these countries, where they're still grown today, the fruit still stays green even when it's fully ripe.

Ever cried while chopping an onion? That's because when you cut one open, you're letting sulphur-rich amino acids meet their enzymes, which were previously separated. It creates a sulphuric chemical that vaporises and can make your eyes sting!

The heat from chillis is caused by a chemical they contain called capsaicin and a chilli's heat is measured on the Scoville scale. Jalapeños can be as hot as 8,000 on the scale, but the world's hottest chilli – the Carolina reaper – has a rating of 2.2 million!

In Southeast Asia, rice is life. It's food. It's culture. It's livelihood. Rice is so important that a common way of asking 'How are you?' in many regional languages is 'Have you eaten rice yet?'. For many generations, the indigenous Ifugao people of the Philippines have etched the exquisite Banaue rice terraces into the mountains.

Tea became a popular drink in China during the Tang and Song dynasties. Making tea involves several steps. First, farmers gather leaves from tea plants and process them by drying then roasting or steaming the leaves. To prepare tea as a drink, you steep the processed leaves in boiling water.

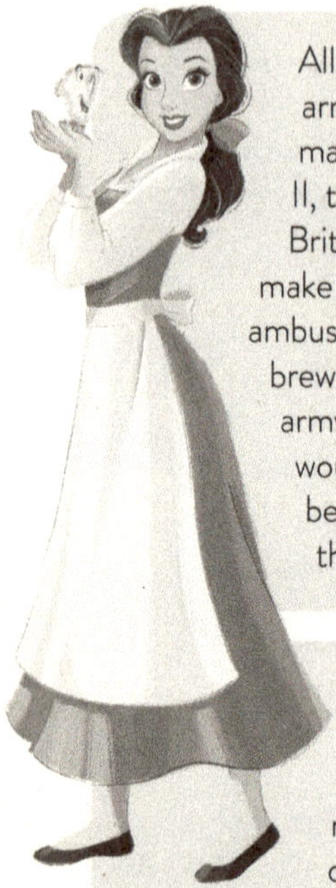

All tanks in the British army are equipped to make tea! In World War II, the story goes that Brits kept stopping to make tea and were often ambushed whilst making a brew. Ever since then, the army chiefs thought it would be a good idea to be able to make tea on the go, inside the tank.

Black, green, white and oolong teas are all the same! They're all derived from the *camellia sinensis* plant, but go through different levels of exposure to oxygen to change their taste and chemical content.

Carrots were originally purple! The orange vegetables that we know today only appeared in the late 16th century, when Dutch growers bred mutated white and yellow carrots to make the common orange version.

The tablecloth wasn't intended to be a covering to protect the table when it was first invented. Instead, it was supposed to be used as a giant napkin for everyone at the table to wipe their messy hands and faces on!

Here's a nutty fact – lots of the things that you think are nuts, actually aren't. The peanut is a legume, more closely related to a bean, while pistachios, cashews and almonds are all seeds. A nut has to have a hard separable shell with a fruit or seed inside, like a Brazil nut.

In 1834, a doctor in Ohio named John Cook started selling a medicine for upset stomachs – tomato ketchup! Ketchup already existed, but it was made out of mushrooms or fish, and Cook's tomato version wasn't used for its current purpose until much later in the 19th century.

Queen Victoria received half a tonne of cheese as a wedding present! Farmers from Somerset donated milk from 700 cows to make the gigantic wheel of cheese, but the Queen turned it down because she liked a more mature variety.

Coronation chicken was created to mark Queen Elizabeth II's ascension to the throne. The United Kingdom's fledgling monarch was honoured by the dish, made using apricots and curried mayonnaise, in 1953.

The people of France eat thousands of tonnes of snails every year! Snails are a French delicacy known as escargot, which is normally prepared with butter and garlic and served as a side dish.

Honey is the only food in the world that doesn't seem to expire. Archaeologists have found jars of honey in Egyptian tombs dating back over 3,000 years, but the runny bee-made nectar is still edible.

The reason mince pies are named as they are is because they used to have minced meat in them! They were less sweet when recipes first appeared in the medieval era and minced meat was added to the fruit and spices we normally have in them today.

The myth that carrots help you see in the dark was created by the British government during World War II to hide the fact that they'd developed radar systems to spot enemy planes. They also wanted to get rid of huge surpluses of the vegetables because they had too many.

In the summers of the Middle Ages, when people were waiting to harvest wheat to make bread, they often had to use old ingredients infected with ergot, which was a fungus that could make you hallucinate!

In the 18th century, John Montagu, the Earl of Sandwich, used to ask his servants to put some meat in between two slices of bread so he could eat and carry on with his day – and the snack we now know as a sandwich has been named after him ever since!

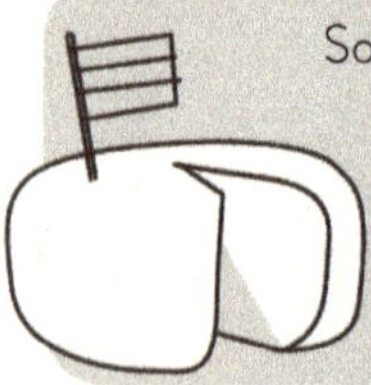

Some areas of Sardinia, Italy, produce a cheese that's illegal in most of the world. It's called casu martzu and the reason it's banned is because it uses live maggots as part of the cheesemaking process... and it is sold with the maggots still inside!

Have you ever heard the phrase 'best thing since sliced bread'? Well, sliced bread was invented in the 1920s, when the Chillicothe Baking Company of Missouri, USA had the bright idea to pre-slice their baked goods. So the next time someone uses that phrase, tell them they actually mean about 100 years ago!

An American company called Beneo launched a product called the Deo Perfume Candy in 2011, which is part sweet, part deodorant. When it's ingested, the sweet releases a rose fragrance through your skin!

McDonalds, the worldwide fast-food chain, once created a broccoli that tasted of bubblegum! It was made by their scientists in an attempt to get kids to eat healthier options, but it never made it to a wide release because testers thought it was too weird!

Figs that grow in the wild are sometimes not suitable for vegetarians. During their pollination process, wasps will burrow into the fruit of a fig tree and lay their eggs inside before dying in the fruit! The fig digests the wasp and eggs before they are ripe enough to be picked.

White chocolate should change its name, because it isn't really chocolate. It has no solid chocolate in it, but gets its name from the cocoa butter that's used to make it, along with sugar, milk and other ingredients. Still tasty though!

Every banana you see is a particular variant called the Cavendish, which was selected precisely because it doesn't have any seeds, so every single one you see is a clone not grown from a seed!

When you eat coriander, it can either taste like a herb or soap! It's all down to your genes, not because you're eating a bad batch of coriander. Some people have a taste receptor that can pick out a particular chemical in coriander that makes them taste of soap instead of a delicious herb!

A bottle of water will have an expiry date on it, but the water can never go out of date! The expiry date is actually for the plastic that the bottle is made from – after a while the chemicals in the plastic will start to degrade and enter the water.

The Caesar salad isn't named after the famous Ancient Roman, nor was it invented anywhere near Italy! It was made by a hotel owner named Caesar Cardini in Tijuana, Mexico when he wanted to feed friends but didn't have much to hand – he threw some bread and dressing on lettuce, and voilà!

# THE WORLD

Blaze a trail across the world and explore every continent on the planet to find out about people and places near and far. These fabulous facts will tell you all about the amazing lands on Earth, the events and people that forged the countries, and show you some of the customs that you might not see outside your front door.

In the early 1920s, mountaineer George Mallory took part in three expeditions to Mount Everest. During an interview, he was asked why he wanted to climb the mountain. 'Because it's there,' he is said to have answered. To many people, this comment sums up the irresistible human urge to explore.

European explorers spent 300 years looking for a sea route between the Atlantic and Pacific Oceans through Canada. They had no idea if it was possible! By breaking sea ice, they were finally able to ram their way through, via a path called the Northwest Passage.

In AD 629, a Chinese Buddhist monk named Xuanzang went on a 17-year journey to learn about Indian Buddhism. He returned with over 600 sacred texts and spent the rest of his life studying and translating them!

Some explorers are looking for natural treasures, such as gold and silver. In the 1500s, King Ferdinand of Spain sent out explorers called conquistadors. Their job was to find precious minerals in the Caribbean and Central America.

A Moroccan scholar named Ibn Battuta logged thirty years and 120,000 kilometres of exploration in the 14th century. Moving by sea, camel caravan and foot, he visited every Muslim nation in the world and many non-Muslim nations as well. When he finally returned home, he described his travels in a book called *The Rihla*, one of the great classics of exploration literature.

In 138 BC, a diplomat named Zhang Qian set out from Chang'an (now Xi'an), the capital of Han dynasty, China, in search of possible allies for a war. His travels spanned decades and revealed unknown regions and goods for trade. His adventures led to the creation of the Silk Road, a network of trade routes across the ancient world.

Sarah Parcak is a modern explorer who uses satellite images to analyse Earth's geology and plant life to reveal forgotten sites. She has found thousands of ancient settlements and over a thousand lost Egyptian tombs working mostly from a computer lab.

Throughout history, animals have set sail on ocean adventures. Cats were kept on board to hunt rats that infested ships, while dogs were used for hunting when the ships came ashore. On one 20th-century Finnish vessel sailors owned pigs, rabbits, a dog and two cats!

In 1831, Charles Darwin joined the crew of the HMS *Beagle*. The ship stopped in the Galápagos Islands off the west coast of South America, where Darwin noticed some unusual traits in the local wildlife. His observations built on his grandfather's work and led to the theory of natural selection, which states that species evolve, changing in response to their surroundings.

It took Krystyna Chojnowska-Liskiewicz 401 days to travel around the world. She set sail from the Canary Islands in a 10-metre yacht, crossing the Atlantic and sailing through the Panama Canal. She crossed the Pacific and Indian Oceans and returned to the Canary Islands on 21 April 1978. She was the first woman to sail around the world alone.

Vikings explored Europe from about AD 790 to 1100. They relied on natural phenomena, such as the Sun and the stars, to find direction and watched for animals such as birds and whales to give them clues to their location. It's possible they used crystals called sunstones to find the Sun in overcast skies, thus helping them to find their way.

In 1519, Portuguese explorer Ferdinand Magellan organised an expedition to find a new route to India, travelling from east to west. It took three years, resulting in the first documented circumnavigation of the Earth.

Cave exploration is called spelunking. Headlamps and spare batteries are very important equipment! Cavers bring harnesses and ropes if they plan to climb inside the cave. They wear helmets, gloves and sturdy boots to protect their heads, hands and feet.

Mount Everest is Earth's highest mountain from sea level. Its peak rises 8,848 metres into the air. Wind speeds of 280 km/h have been recorded at the summit and temperatures can drop as low as −60°C. As of 2023, over 6,300 adventurers have stood on the mountain's summit.

Earth's surface has many remote spots that remain unexplored. Northern Greenland, most of Antarctica and the deserts of Namibia in Africa are still unknown. People have never set foot on many mountaintops and the dense Amazon rainforest still has many untouched areas. There is plenty of exploring left to do on our planet.

When explorers came to new areas, they often brought diseases. Local people had never been exposed to these illnesses, so they had no natural immunity and no medicines to fight them. Between the years 1500 and 1900, an estimated 90 percent of North America's native population died from European diseases like smallpox, measles, bubonic plague, influenza and others.

In Micronesia, early explorers trained using a stick chart, which mapped where islands and currents were. Wayfinders used their eyes and ears and studied the ocean for years. They remembered what they learned and passed their knowledge on, often through song.

Over 90 percent of the sea floor is unexplored! Many incredible natural features and countless new plant and animal species are sure to be down there.

There's a place in Venezuela that has thunderstorms for up to 300 nights a year! It occurs where the Catatumbo River feeds into Lake Maracaibo, bringing the cold air from the mountains to meet the warm air of the Caribbean Sea.

A tribe called the Uros live on the surface of Lake Titicaca in Peru, on islands they created. They made the islands from the totora reeds that grow from the lake, and they also built their houses and boats from the same material!

In 1911, American explorer Hiram Bingham III went to Peru looking for a place called Vilcabamba. He found a forgotten city called Machu Picchu instead. The 'Lost City', as this mountaintop retreat is sometimes called, had sat empty for hundreds of years after its residents died or left. Today, this spectacular spot is Peru's most popular tourist attraction.

People in Peru farm salt! Over 600 families in the region of Sacred Valley own the Maras Salt Mines, which is a collection of saltwater pools connected by canals. When the sun shines, the pools dry out and the families harvest the salt left behind.

The Amazon River, the second biggest river in the world, begins in the Andes mountain range in Peru. It flows through the rainforest and is home to loads of weird and wonderful animals including the electric eel, pink river dolphin and piranhas!

The Mountain of Seven Colours, also known as Vinicunca, is a multicoloured mountain found in the Peruvian Andes. It was only discovered to contain so many colours in 2015 when the snow that had always covered it melted away.

South America consists of 12 sovereign states and 3 non-sovereign dependent territories, from Venezuela in the north to Chile on the southern tip. All but two of them have access to the sea – Paraguay and Bolivia are both landlocked, though the Amazon runs through both.

Brazil has been the largest producer of coffee beans for over 150 years! The massive country harvested over 2.5 million tonnes of coffee in 2016 alone!

One of Bolivia's most famous hotspots is the Salar de Uyuni, known in English as the Uyuni Salt Flats. The land there is covered by a layer of salt and when it rains, the ground turns into a gigantic mirror as far as the eye can see!

There's another giant river in South America besides the Amazon – and it actually runs underneath it. Rio Hamza, an unofficial name, is an underground waterway that runs 4 kilometres below the surface of the Amazon and flows almost vertically in places.

In Paraguay, you don't have to ring a doorbell to announce your arrival at someone's home. Instead, you can just clap for a few seconds until somebody lets you inside.

Venezuela was named by an explorer called Amerigo Vespucci, who landed in the area at the end of the 15th century. He likened the stilt villages of the country to the waterlogged city of Venice and called it Veneziola, which means 'little Venice'. The Spanish translation is Venezuela.

The Amazon rainforest is home to over 1.5 million indigenous people, spread across over 300 different ethnic groups. It's believed that the groups that live in just the Brazilian Amazon collectively speak over 250 different languages.

The capital of Brazil, Brasília, was purposely built to be the capital city in the 1950s to move some of the country's functions to the centre of the huge land. It took just over three years to build it from the ground up and it was designed to look like a plane if viewed from above.

Christ the Redeemer is a massive 30-metre-tall landmark of Jesus Christ that sits atop a mountain in Rio de Janeiro. It looms more than 700 metres above the city and was originally built in France before being sent to Brazil to be assembled piece by piece, opening in 1931.

Colombia is home to a rainbow river, known as Caño Cristales, or the River of Five Colours. The water in the river is affected by the plant life inside it, which occasionally changes the flow to yellow, orange, blue or green.

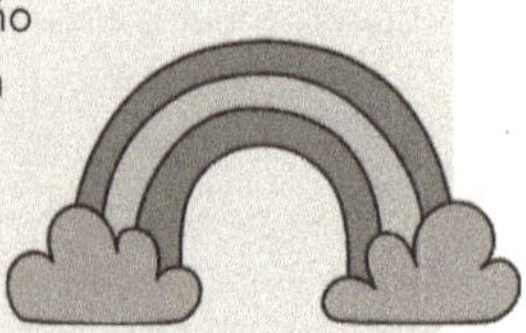

There's a popular hobby in Colombia called tejo, which involves throwing metal discs into a clay pit. The twist is that the clay pit is filled with 'landmines' made from gunpowder that will explode when you hit them.

Brazil is so massive – it's the fifth largest country in the world by size – that it borders all but two of the other countries in South America. Only Chile and Ecuador are unable to call the nation a neighbour.

Ushuaia, Argentina, is the world's most southern city, only accessible by flight from mainland Argentina. It's a popular holiday destination for snowsports and hiking and you can often see hundreds of whales in migration around the island city.

By law, Colombian radio stations are required to play the country's national anthem on air twice a day! Tune your radio to any of Colombia's stations at 6 in either the morning or the evening and you'll hear its patriotic song from your speakers.

Pope Francis I, who began his papacy as leader of the Catholic Church in 2013, was born in Buenos Aires, Argentina in 1936. But before he became the first South American Pope, he worked as a bouncer at an Argentinian nightclub in his home city.

There's a small settlement of Welsh descendants in the middle of remote Argentina. It's called Y Wladfa and was created when people from Wales emigrated from their homeland in 1865 because they feared the language and culture of Wales was under threat from the English.

The national sport of Argentina – home of Maradona and Messi – isn't football, but a game called Pato. It's played on horseback and involves throwing a hoop-covered ball around and trying to get it in a small netted basket.

Guyana's name means 'the land of many waterfalls' – it has over 300 of the aquatic sites in one of the smallest South American countries. It has the highest single-drop waterfall in the world, the Kaieteur Falls, which falls non-stop from a cliff 250 metres high!

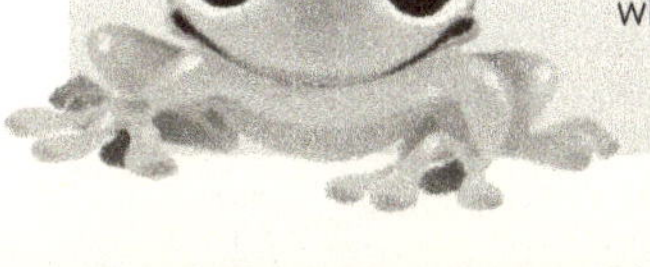

Mexico has 31 states and about 129 million people. Mexico City, the nation's capital, has almost 9 million residents. The Mexican flag is green, white and red and has a central image that shows an eagle eating a snake while landing on the nopal cactus.

The Aztec civilisation flourished from 1300 to 1521. Aztecs were highly skilled engineers who built bridges, aqueducts and artificial islands called chinampas. Nahuatl, the Aztec language, is spoken widely throughout Mexico today.

Kīlauea in Hawai'i is one of our planet's most extreme volcanoes. This volcano erupted continuously from 1983, finally ending on 4 September 2018, after 35 straight years of oozing lava.

Between May 1804 and September 1806, the Lewis and Clark Expedition became the first European expedition to cross what is now the western United States. A Lemhi Shoshone woman named Sacagawea travelled with the expedition most of the way, translating conversations when the expedition met Indiginous Americans. Her presence put people at ease, since war parties rarely included women.

Scholars refer to the historical and cultural region formed by Mexico and Central America as Mesoamerica. Many groups, tribes and kingdoms created important civilisations in this region and five major ones formed the foundation of modern Mexico. These are the Olmec, the Teotihuacan (tee-oh-tee-wah-KAHN), the Toltec, the Aztec and the Maya.

The people who live in Mexico have many origins. Some are indigenous to the land, such as the Aztec and Maya people. Other Mexicans are descendants of Europeans, while some also have African or Asian roots. The word mestizo is used in Latin America to describe people of blended heritage.

Geologists call the area along the edges of the Pacific Ocean the Ring of Fire. Here, tectonic plates, or huge pieces of the Earth's crust, rub against one another. The movement can trigger tremors, major earthquakes and volcanic eruptions. Mexico, the USA and many other countries lie on the Ring of Fire.

The ancient Maya people of Mexico made incredible advances in mathematics, astronomy and architecture. They were one of the civilisations to develop the concept of zero and also discovered that Earth takes about 365 days to go around the sun. The Maya built complex cities and created beautiful works of art.

Many families in Mexico create ofrendas in their homes or at cemeteries during Dia de Muertos. An ofrenda consists of at least three levels. The top level represents heaven. The middle of the ofrenda stands for Earth. The lower level is Mictlan, meaning the 'Land of the Dead'.

Mammoth Cave in Kentucky, USA, is the world's longest cave system. About 680 kilometres of the system has been explored. But there may be another 960 kilometres still undiscovered! Today the cave is managed by the US National Park Service.

A waterfall is a place where water flows over one large vertical drop or a series of shorter steep drops. Waterfalls can be short and small, or they can be huge. Horseshoe Falls, which is part of the Niagara Falls series on the USA-Canada border, is 820 metres wide and its roaring waters plunge 51 metres!

Mexico has 9,330 kilometres of ocean coastline and some of the most beautiful beaches in the world. Mexicans and visitors from around the world flock to the beaches all year. Cancún, Los Cabos, Playa del Carmen and Acapulco are home to many popular beaches.

Martin Van Buren was the eighth president of the USA, but the first to be born an American! All the previous presidents had been Englishmen as they were born before America won independence in 1776.

Popocatépetl (poh-poh-kah-TEH-peh-tuhl) and Iztaccihuatl (ee-stahk-SEE-wah-tuhl) are two famous active volcanoes located outside Mexico City. In the Nahuatl (nah-WAH-tuhl) language, Popocatépetl means 'smoking mountain' and Iztaccihuatl means 'white lady'. Some Mexicans call the volcanoes El Popo and Izta for short.

Mexico has no official language, and at least 63 indigenous ones. Nahuatl is spoken by more than a million modern Mexicans. Many common English words derive from Nahuatl, including avocado, chocolate and coyote. Yucatec Maya, Mixtec and Zapotec are just a few of the other indigenous languages commonly spoken in Mexico.

The Mississippi River is the third longest in the world and the longest in America, measuring 3,765 kilometres! It would take a drop of water travelling from its source over 90 days to reach the end of its journey.

Baffin Island in Canada is home to the world's highest vertical drop. The steep fall is from a ledge on Thor Peak and you would fall 1,250 metres before hitting the floor. Most high mountains slope upwards so they don't have such high drops like this.

Mexicans celebrate the country's independence from Spain on 16 September. People throughout the country celebrate with music, parades and fireworks. The Grito, or cry for independence, is another part of the celebration, which commemorates a priest named Miguel Hidalgo y Costilla, who made the call for independence in 1810.

Dia de Muertos begins on 3 October and lasts through to 2 November. The important celebration has its roots in Aztec tradition and is one of the most deeply revered customs in Mexico. The holiday honours ancestors and loved ones who have passed away.

The hottest place on Earth is Death Valley in the USA. The national park, which straddles the states of Nevada and California, set the record in 1913 when it hit a temperature of 56.6°C! It still regularly reaches over 48°C!

Teotihuacan, an ancient city near Mexico City, was built more than two thousand years ago and had running water, a sewer system, living quarters and courtyards. The Pyramid of the Sun and the Pyramid of the Moon, which were built to line up with the sunrises and sunsets at certain times of the year, are the largest structures in the city. But scientists still don't know who built it!

Each object on an ofrenda has a special meaning. Candles and marigold petals guide the spirits of loved ones to the altar. Copal incense is burned to purify the souls of the spirits. Pan de muerto and other favourite foods are offered as a way to honour loved ones.

The Maya people built Chichén Itzá (chee-CHEN-eet-ZAH) more than 1,000 years ago. The city includes a stone-lined field where the Maya played sports. The city's Pyramid of Kukulcan has broad steps that appear as if the serpent god Kukulcan is climbing the steps when shadows are cast over them at certain points. In *Coco*, Miguel sees similar steps and pyramids in the Land of the Dead!

The Statue of Liberty in New York was a present from France. It was given by the French as a token of their alliance with Americans against the British during the American Revolution.

Vatican City, home of the Catholic Church, is the smallest country in the world. It's home to just over 800 residents and is entirely landlocked by the city of Rome in Italy.

The New London Bridge was sold 136 years after it was built, when it was dismantled, shipped to the USA and reassembled over Lake Havasu. The Modern London Bridge that crosses the Thames now was opened in 1973.

In 1888, a team led by Norwegian explorer Fridtjof Nansen made the first crossing of Greenland's frozen interior – on cross-country skis! The 450-kilometre journey took six weeks. The team faced bone-chilling cold, constant snowstorms and icy crevasses along the way. Amazingly, no one was seriously hurt on this ambitious adventure.

Stonehenge, in the county of Wiltshire in England, is one of the oldest man-made landmarks in the world. It dates back to around 3000 BC and is made of 4-metre-tall stones arranged in a circle, which seem to align with the sunrise on the longest day of the year!

The Ancient Greeks built statues and temples for their various gods so they had a place to worship them. The most famous of these is the Parthenon in Athens, which was built for the goddess of wisdom and war, Athena, who is also the protector of Greece's capital city.

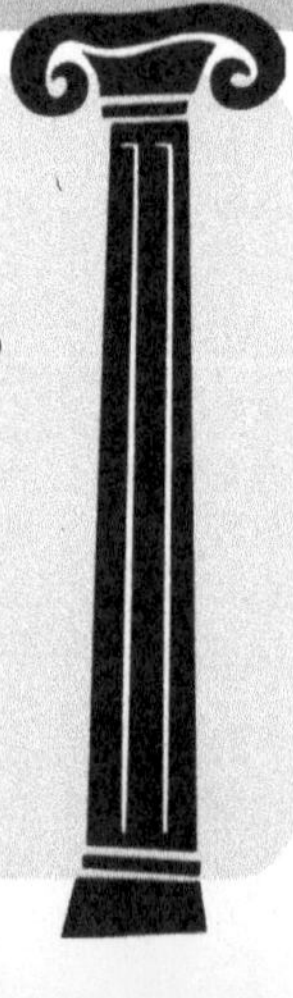

One of the oldest parliaments in the world is in Iceland, where it has governed the people of the tiny nation for over a thousand years! The Althing was created in AD 930 and has remained the seat of power ever since.

The Tower of London in England is home to six ravens at any one time. There's a superstition that if any fewer than six are present then the monarchy in the country will fall!

As one of the oldest universities in the world, Oxford University in the UK is even older than the Aztec Empire! Oxford welcomed its first students in AD 1096, but the founding of the city of Tenochtitlán, the start of the Aztec Empire, wasn't until over 200 years later, in 1325.

The Leaning Tower of Pisa has never been straight! The Italian landmark started to tilt when it was being built due to soft ground on one side, but the constructors continued adding floors until they were finished.

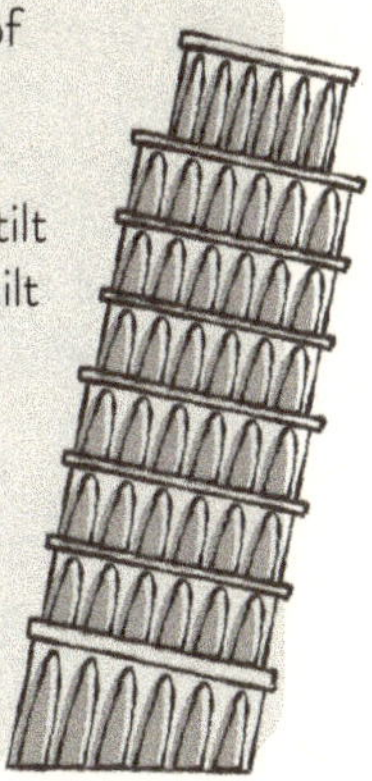

The abandoned Bolshoi Zayatsky island in Russia's White Sea is dotted with mysterious stone labyrinths. Archaeologists are not sure of the labyrinths' function, but it seems they had a spiritual purpose. Different experts believe ancient peoples may have built them as doors to the underworld, traps for evil spirits, or altars for religious rituals. However, some experts think they may have just been designs for fishing equipment.

The principality of Monaco, a tiny country surrounded by France, has more people in its military orchestra than it does in the actual military! There are 85 musicians in the orchestra, while only 82 people serve as a member of their armed forces.

There's a town in Germany called Nördlingen, which is built entirely within the crater left by a meteor impact. The crater is called the Nördlinger Ries and is the result of an impact over 14 million years ago!

The Czech Republic's, or Czechia's, capital city Prague has a street that's so narrow that people have gotten stuck in it. Vinárna Čertovka is only 50 centimetres wide and has traffic lights at each end to let people know when they can walk through it!

The Greek regions of Athens and Sparta were at war in the 5th century BC for 27 years, but a peace treaty wasn't signed between the two areas until AD 1996, when the modern mayors decided to do the official paperwork to end the conflict!

The recycling systems in Sweden are so effective that the country often runs out of rubbish to process. However, they burn waste that can't be recycled to create energy, so they have to import trash from Norway to keep their energy grid going!

The modern reconstruction of Shakespeare's Globe, which lies on the south bank of the Thames, is the only building in London that is allowed to have a thatched roof, after such roofs were blamed for the immense spread of the Great Fire of London in 1666.

Lots of towns and cities have multiple twins across the world, but Paris and Rome are exclusive twins, and they even have a shared motto: 'Only Paris is worthy of Rome; only Rome is worthy of Paris'. How romantic!

There's a prison island in Norway where inmates can freely roam around and do whatever they want. It sounds strange, but this approach to punishment has led to the lowest levels of re-offending criminals in the world.

Visitors from Japan to France's capital are sometimes sent into a state of shock known as Paris Syndrome. It happens when the tourists discover that Paris isn't as wonderful as they've seen in the media or it isn't what they expected!

Warsaw, the capital city of Poland, was burned to the ground in 1944, a year before World War II ended. But thanks to the detailed paintings of Bernardo Bellotto, the Polish people were able to rebuild its capital to its former glory almost exactly.

In 1963, a man in Turkey knocked down a wall in his house, which opened up a hole into a strange room. This unusual discovery got even weirder when he discovered this room led to a place called Derinkuyu, an ancient underground city that could date back to 1500 BC!

The British monarchy is the most famous in the world, but ten different European countries still have one! Andorra, Belgium, Lichtenstein, the Netherlands, Norway, Spain and Sweden all have one, but Denmark's is the oldest, dating back to the 10th century BC.

If you live in the United Kingdom, the King of England himself will send you a birthday card when you turn 100! He'll carry on sending you a birthday card every five years, or an anniversary card if you've been married for 65, 70 or 75 years!

La Sagrada Familia is a church being built in Barcelona, Spain based on a design by Antoni Gaudí, a famous Spanish artist. It started construction in 1882, but it's so complicated that it's still being constructed, almost 100 years after Gaudí died in 1926!

Known as the golden age, China's Tang dynasty was a time of peace and prosperity. The Chinese traded silk, spices, tea and other valuable items with Central Asian and some European countries along the Silk Road. Literature, especially poetry, also thrived. Over 50,000 poems written during this period survive to the present.

Many Chinese dynasties lasted hundreds of years. Others did not last long at all, like the Qin Dynasty, which was only in power for 15 years. The filmmakers who worked on the *Mulan* movie were particularly inspired by the Han and Tang dynasties.

Shan Yu is a fictional character in *Mulan*, but threats of invasion in China's history were real. The Great Wall was originally built to prevent northern tribes from invading China. Workers used stone, brick, earth and wood to build the structure. Watchtowers and garrisons were built along the wall to help guard the border.

China is a country located on the continent of Asia. One of the world's oldest civilisations, the Chinese are responsible for many important inventions and discoveries. Today, over 1.4 billion people live in China. It has the largest population of any country in the world.

The Four Great Ancient Capitals of China are Beijing, Nanjing, Luoyang and Xi'an. Luoyang and Xi'an were capitals during the Han and Tang dynasties. There are many ancient temples and buildings still standing in these cities.

The idea to build the Great Wall of China came from Qin Shi Huang, who was the first emperor of the Qin dynasty (221–206 BC). The size and length of the wall changed over the centuries, as dynasties extended, strengthened, and rebuilt the wall. The Great Wall that still stands today was mostly built during the Ming dynasty (1368–1644). It stretches for about 8,850 kilometres.

Starting in 1420, China's emperor lived and ruled in the Forbidden City. Located in Beijing, the palace was 'forbidden' to commoners. The Forbidden City was made up of 980 buildings where government officials lived and helped the emperor make important decisions.

Chinese New Year is celebrated on the first new moon of the lunar calendar. The holiday usually lands between 21 January and 20 February in the Gregorian calendar and families celebrate the occasion for many days. They wear red clothing, have family dinners and give red envelopes filled with money to children, as red is considered a lucky colour in China.

Southeast Asia consists of 11 countries: Brunei, Cambodia, Indonesia, Laos, Malaysia, Myanmar, the Philippines, Singapore, Thailand, Timor-Leste and Vietnam. The population of Southeast Asia is almost 700 million people and growing!

Filial piety is one teaching of a belief system called Confucianism. Confucius was a teacher who lived from 551 to 479 BC. Confucius believed that society worked like a family. Just as children obeyed and respected their elders, all people had to obey and respect the emperor. Even today, Confucianism has a strong influence on Chinese society.

China has over 30,000 unique species of animals and plants. Species that are endemic to China do not naturally live or grow anywhere else in the world.

The Qingming Festival is a holiday dedicated to remembering and honouring ancestors. The holiday, which takes place in early April, has been celebrated in China for over 2,500 years. On this day, families visit their ancestors' graves to clean them and present special offerings. They also light scented sticks called incense and burn joss paper, which represents money.

The Southeast Asian islands are home to Brunei and Timor-Leste, as well as several archipelagos, or chains of islands, that make up Indonesia, the Philippines and Malaysia. Composed of over 17,000 islands, the Indonesian archipelago is the largest in the world. Beautiful beaches, vibrant coral reefs, and active volcanoes are key features of the islands.

The Minangkabau of Sumatra, Indonesia, is considered by many scholars to be the largest matrilineal society in the world. In their tradition, Minangkabau daughters inherit their families' homes through their mothers. In many cases, when a daughter marries, her husband moves in with her family.

The oldest city in the world that has been constantly inhabited is Damascus in Syria. The ancient dwelling, known as the Jasmine City, is the capital of the country and was first inhabited over 11,000 years ago.

Over 20 percent of Earth's animal, plant and marine species live in Southeast Asia. Indonesia, Malaysia and the Philippines contain so many varieties of species that they are classified as megadiverse!

The mainland of Southeast Asia is part of the larger Asian continent and consists of Cambodia, Laos, Myanmar, Thailand, Vietnam, Singapore and the peninsula portion of Malaysia. Here you'll see long mountain ranges that fan out into lowlands and flat areas called plateaus. You'll also marvel at breathtaking karst formations made from layers of rocks such as limestone.

Cambodia's Angkor Wat is the world's largest temple complex and is one of the most visited religious sites in the world. Built by the Khmer Empire 1,000 years ago, the 'temple city' covers over 161 hectares and was carved from rock made of compacted sand, known as sandstone.

Your eyes aren't playing tricks on you. Rivers can flow backwards! At Cambodia's Tonlé Sap, Southeast Asia's largest lake, a special event occurs during the summer months. The flow of water reverses direction, moving away from the sea, filling the Tonlé Sap with much-needed fish and providing water for nearby crops.

Borobudur temple in Java, Indonesia, is considered the largest Buddhist temple in the world. A few hundred years older than Angkor Wat, the structure is shaped like a stepped pyramid and stands over 30 metres tall. Hundreds of bell-shaped stupas, or places of meditation, and Buddha statues can be found around the temple.

Most of Southeast Asia is close to Earth's equator, in the humid tropics region. The subtropics to the north and south have hot summers and mild winters, so Southeast Asia is blanketed in lush forests, deserts and snowy mountains. Mũi Né in Vietnam is famous for stunning desert dunes, and Puncak Jaya in Indonesia is so tall, it even snows there!

For over a thousand years from around 300 BC, India was the only known source of diamonds in the world. It wasn't until AD 1700 that more diamond deposits were found in places like Brazil in South America and South Africa.

Did you know that languages from three major families are spoken in Southeast Asia? Languages like Lao and Thai are members of the Kra–Dai language family. They are tonal, which means they utilise the relative highness or lowness of sounds, called pitch, to completely change the meaning of a word. Austronesian languages are spoken on the islands, including the Philippines, Indonesia and Malaysia. Austroasiatic languages like Vietnamese and Cambodia's Khmer are spoken on the mainland.

The tallest statue in the world is the Statue of Unity, which is found in India and measures 182 metres tall! It's almost twice as big as the Statue of Liberty and shows a local independence leader named Sardar Vallabhbhai Patel.

The loudest sound ever recorded was the eruption of the volcano Krakatoa in 1883. It exploded on the Indonesian island and damaged the ears of people up to 64 kilometres away. It was even heard 3,000 kilometres away in Mauritius.

During the dry season in Luang Prabang, Laos, locals come together to build bridges over rivers. Made from bamboo and rope alone, these useful bridges connect towns to schools, businesses and markets. Then, before the wet season, locals dismantle the bridges so they're not washed away by strong currents.

India has 300,000 mosques and over 3 million Hindu temples. It's not surprising given the country is the second most populated country in the world, but that's a lot of worship! The holy city of Varanasi has over 23,000 temples alone.

The continent of Africa is so huge that it's the only one in the world that has parts in each of the four hemispheres (north, south, east and west). For example, South Africa is in the southern and eastern hemispheres, while Morocco is in the northern and western ones.

When you think of the pyramids, you think of the ones in Egypt, right? Well, it's not even the country with the most pyramids in Africa. Egypt has 138 of the pointy triangles, but Sudan has discovered 255 of them!

The pyramids that are found in Egypt are all tombs of the country's ancient,rulers, known as pharaohs – they're all basically monumental graves! Bodies of the pharaohs would be mummified and buried in a sarcophagus, which is a grand ornamental coffin.

The River Nile runs through 11 different countries, including Egypt, Eritrea and Sudan. It has two small rivers, known as tributaries, that flow into it – the White Nile, from Burundi and the Blue Nile from Ethiopia. The rivers meet in Sudan.

The Sahara Desert, which covers large parts of North Africa such as Egypt, Algeria and Chad, is the largest warm desert in the world. The only bigger deserts are the cold ones at the poles – the Antarctic and Arctic. The Sahara Desert is bigger than the USA!

Because there are over 50 countries in Africa, the languages spoken differ all over the continent. Arabic is the most common one, used in Egypt for example, but there are over 2,000 languages spoken across Africa.

Before settlers arrived in Africa and colonised the territory, the continent was divided into over 10,000 different states and settlements. Each one had its customs and possibly its own language, which is why Africa is so diverse, even within countries.

Africa is home to the world's oldest university: the University of al-Qarawiyyin. It was established in Fez, a city in Morocco around AD 859, which was 200 years before Europe's first university – the University of Bologna in Italy opened in AD 1088.

Some Tunisians believe that fish ward off evil spirits from homes, so they often hang pictures of fish in their house to keep their families safe. Others even put fish bones in the structure of their house, placed in the walls or floors.

The earliest known human fossils have been discovered on the continent of Africa, which has led scientists to believe that all humans originated from Africa. The human remains found in Africa date back to around 7 million years ago.

On the border between Zambia and Zimbabwe, you'll find the Victoria Falls, which is the largest waterfall in Africa. Its drop descends over 108 metres and stretches across over 1.6 kilometres along the border between the countries.

If you want to reach the highest point in Africa, you'll need to travel to Mount Kilimanjaro in Tanzania. It's one of the tallest mountains in the world, reaching up to 5,894 metres above sea level, and over a thousand people are rescued attempting to climb the tricky trek every year.

The most populated African country is Nigeria, which is home to over 218 million people. It's a massive and diverse country that has over 500 different languages, such as Yoruba and Igbo.

Madagascar is an island country that lies off the Eastern coast of the African mainland. It's the fourth largest island in the world and the biggest belonging to Africa – it's over 1,600 kilometres long and 563 kilometres wide.

There's a tribe in the south of the continent called the San, who are said to be direct descendants of the first homo sapiens, or humans. They're the oldest known tribe in Africa and have lived in places like Namibia and South Africa for over 20,000 years!

Africa is home to the tallest, fastest and biggest land animals in the world – the giraffe, cheetah and African elephant – as well as very unexpected creatures. African penguins can be found on the South African coast, though they're an endangered species.

In Saudi Arabia they have dust devils – small whirlwinds that pick up dust and sand – although they know them by another name: djin. It's an Arabic word that means genie or devil, and is the reason why genies are typically shown without legs.

The world's first zoo could have been opened more than 5,500 years ago! Archaeologists discovered the skeletons of 112 animals, including elephants, hippos and wildcats, buried in an ancient structure at Hierakonpolis in Egypt.

Lebanon has a multicultural rule that states their three highest government positions must be held by people of different faiths. The president must be a Christian, the speaker of the Lebanese parliament must be a Sunni Muslim, while the prime minister should be a Shi'a Muslim.

There's a strip of land between Egypt and Sudan called Bir Tawil, which is perfectly good land that neither country wants to claim as their own. Instead, both of them lay claim to a nearby piece of land known as the Halaib Triangle, a much bigger part of land on the east coast of Africa between the two countries.

If you're born in Benin, you're more likely to be a twin than anywhere else in the world. The African country reports 27 twins out of every one thousand births, which is almost double the global average!

Napoleon's invasion of Egypt is the reason we know so much about the Ancient civilisation. He brought with him a commission of the sciences and arts, which documented everything they saw in the country.

When the grasslands of Namibia sprout up, they're often dotted with unexplained 'fairy circles' – bare patches of ground surrounded by tall grass. Scientists have studied over 1,500 kilometres of land where this happens and still don't know the reason behind them.

Over half of the gold that's ever been mined on Earth has come from South Africa, and from one particular mine in Witwatersrand. South Africa is also famed for its diamonds, and the continent produces half of the world's diamonds too.

Ethiopia has its own calendar called the Ge'ez Calendar, which has 13 months compared to the 12 that we have in the Western calendar. They add five or six days into the 13th month, so their years are slightly longer and the calendar runs behind – in 2023, the Ge'ez Calendar was still in 2016!

Cowry shells were used as currency all along the West African coast and their influence can still be seen today. The currency of Ghana is cedi, which is a Ghanaian word that translates as cowry shell.

The first Black African to win an Olympic medal came from Ethiopia. Abebe Bikila won the marathon event in 1960 in Rome and he did it barefoot! He won the gold medal again four years later in Tokyo, but wore trainers that time.

Liberia is Africa's oldest surviving country, declaring itself independent in 1847, more than half a century before the next African country, South Africa, did the same thing. It was one of only two countries in Africa not to be colonised by Europeans, along with Ethiopia.

There's an island off the coast of Mozambique called... Mozambique. The island is a UNESCO World Heritage site – the only one in the country – and home to the oldest European church in the Southern Hemisphere, which dates back to the 1500s.

Senegal's Pink Lake has a special algae in it that turns the water a cloudy shade of pink and also makes it very salty. The lake can be up to 40 percent salt and the Senegalese people who mine the salt underwater cover themselves in shea butter to protect them from the harsh waters!

The Burj Khalifa, which is in the city of Dubai in the United Arab Emirates, is the tallest building in the world. It took the record when it was finished in 2009 and from top to bottom, it measures 829.8 metres tall!

The whole of the Middle East covers about the same amount of land as the USA – 9 million square kilometres to be precise. The largest country is Saudi Arabia and the smallest is Bahrain.

A writer from Syria in the 2nd century AD wrote a book called *True History*, which predicted many events of the future. Lucian of Samosata's adventure featured people going to the moon, encountering aliens and finding a new land in the West, which could have been North America!

Although Saudi Arabia has vast deserts full of sand, they still import tons of the stuff from Australia. Not to refill the desert, of course, but to use when building houses and other constructions, as the Saudi sand isn't fit for this purpose.

Three men from Yemen sued NASA in 1997 for trespassing on Mars with their *Sojourner* rover. The men had supposedly inherited the planet from their ancestors more than 3,000 years ago and had the paperwork to prove it!

The tiny gerbils we keep as pets were first found in Syria in 1797. The vegetable-munching creatures were first sent around the world in 1930 when a zoologist sent them to labs to be used in medical research.

In 2007, scientists who were digging up fossils in Saudi Arabia uncovered the remains of a huge fungus that would've reached up to 9 metres tall! The fungi died out over 350 million years ago, but would've covered Saudi Arabia in a forest of mushroom-like trees.

Israel is the only Middle Eastern country to appear in the Eurovision Song Contest! It normally hosts entrants just from Europe, but Israel has been a competitor in the annual singing competition since 1973. Other non-European countries to have taken part include Cyrpus and Australia.

There's a place called Baba Gurgur in Iraq that has a phenomenon known as the Eternal Fire, where a flame has been blazing for thousands of years. It's caused by natural gas seeping out of rocks in the ground, but nobody knows what first set it alight.

The Dead Sea, which is on the border of Jordan is the lowest land-based elevation at 430 metres below sea level. It's more than nine times saltier than the sea, which means that life can barely survive in or around it, which is where it gets its name from.

Ancient Mesopotamia, which used to exist where the Middle East is now, was known as the land between two rivers – Tigris and Euphrates, which still run through the region today. They both begin in the Turkish mountains and flow through Iraq, Syria, Iran and Kuwait.

Kuwait is currently planning to build the world's tallest building: the Burj Mubarak Al-Kabir, which it expects to complete in 2048. It will be 1,001 metres high, which is a tribute to the popular story treasury *One Thousand and One Nights*.

The Caribbean is made up of over 700 different islands. Only around a hundred of these are inhabited, however, and 70 percent of Caribbean people live on the island of Cuba, or the island that contains Haiti and the Dominican Republic.

The shortest airport runway in the world is on the island of Saba, north of Saint Kitts and Nevis in the Caribbean. Pilots have just 400 metres in which to land and stop their plane when they make a landing here.

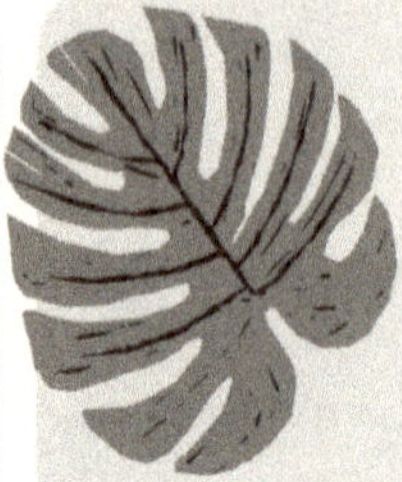

Ian Fleming, the author of the James Bond novels, loved Jamaica so much that he bought land and built a house there called Goldeneye, after one of his stories. He wrote all of the James Bond books from his Caribbean property.

The Central American country of Costa Rica doesn't have an army. It hasn't had one since the military program ended in 1949 after a civil war. Instead, the money was used to fund education throughout the land.

Although they're thousands of kilometres away from Europe, the islands of Guadeloupe, Martinique and Saint Martin are all technically part of the European Union. They're part of the French overseas territory even though they're in the Caribbean, so you can spend Euros there.

There's a lake on the island of Dominica that is not fit for a swim as it's constantly boiling! The water sits on top of a fumarole – a vent to a volcano that shoots out boiling hot gases – which makes the water hot and bubbly all the time!

The Nicoya region in the western part of Costa Rica is one of five so-called 'blue zones' in the world. Some think that people in these blue zones are more likely to reach 100 years of age than anywhere else in the world due to their healthy lifestyles.

Like many countries in Central and South America, Nicaragua doesn't have any street names. It can be confusing to get around, but Nicaraguan people give directions based on landmarks like buildings rather than road names.

Lots of countries celebrate independence days, but Panama has two special occasions. They celebrate their independence from Spain, which was gained in 1821, and from Colombia, which happened in 1903.

Off the coast of Belize, there's a beautiful deep blue circle in the middle of the crystal clear waters. Known as the Great Blue Hole, it's a giant flooded sinkhole that has stalactites inside it, which suggests it was a cave when the sea level was lower.

The Panama Canal is a man-made crossing over the country of Panama that was built to speed up voyages across the sea by cutting through the narrow nation. Every ship that passes through must pay a toll, with the largest ships paying over $450,000 to cross.

Jamaica is the only country in the world that has a flag combining green, gold and black and each colour has a different meaning. Black stands for difficulties in the country's past, green represents agriculture and gold signifies the year-round tropical sun!

The Pacific Islands are divided into three groups: Melanesia, which means 'black islands'; Micronesia, which means 'small islands'; and Polynesia, which means 'many islands'. The suffix -nesia comes from a Greek word that means 'island'.

We don't always know the exact dates and times for events from the past in the Pacific Islands, because history wasn't written down as it is now. Instead, tales were told out loud by storytellers like Gramma Tala in *Moana*. These storytellers passed the stories down to their children and their children's children, which is known as oral history.

There are giant head statues called mo'ai on Rapa Nui, which is also known as Easter Island. The mo'ai were carved hundreds of years ago and measure up to 10 metres high, even though large parts of the statue are buried underground.

Two of the last islands to be settled are in Polynesia: Hawai'i at the top and New Zealand at the bottom. The first settlers travelled over 3,000 kilometres by canoe to reach Hawai'i. Early Pacific settlers made an even longer trip to New Zealand, about 1,200 years ago. They named their home Aotearoa, which is still used today.

Two of the countries in Polynesia are Samoa and Tonga. People have lived on these islands for more than 3,000 years. Samoa means 'sacred centre'. Tonga is made up of 171 islands. Fewer than half of the islands in Tonga have people on them.

In Tonga and Samoa, a house is called a fale. Early Samoans and Tongans built fales using only what they had on the island – wood from poumuli trees held up a roof made of coconut leaves sewn together with rope made of – you guessed it – coconut! Fales are still made in this way today.

There is a monument in Tonga called Ha'amonga 'a Maui, which translates to 'Burden of Maui'. The monument is made of three huge stone slabs, each weighing more than 30 tonnes! It is almost a thousand years old and may have been built to measure time using the sun.

The small island nation of Nauru is the only country in the world that doesn't have a proper capital city. There is a city called Yaren, where the country's parliament runs the country from, but they haven't named it their capital city in law!

Uluru is a giant monolith – a single massive stone that stands on its own – in the Northern Territory of Australia. It's the biggest monolith in the entire world and is the sandstone remnants of an ancient mountain range. Uluru is sacred to Pitjantjatjara, the Aboriginal people of the area, known as the Aṉangu.

There's a fence in Australia that stretches for 5,614 kilometres. It stretches from the town of Jimbour in the east of the country, to the Nullarbor Plain in the south and was put up to stop dingoes from reaching farmland in the southeast of the country.

The Marquesas Islands have many petroglyphs, which are drawings on rocks. There are drawings of turtles, canoes and people, but nobody has any idea how old they are.

Oceania is the smallest continent on the planet by land area, which is why it's named after the waters in between the many islands. It's also the least populated of the continents apart from Antarctica.

Oceania contains almost two-thirds of the planet's marsupials – mammals that carry their babies in pouches – such as koalas, wombats and kangaroos. The only other place you can find marsupials is South America.

Oceania is the only place in the world where you can find a monotreme – a mammal that lays eggs. In fact, there are just two monotremes in the world: the duck-billed platypus and the echidna, and both call Oceania home.

Only six cities in the whole of Oceania have a population of over a million people. Five of these are in Australia, including Sydney, Melbourne and Brisbane, while Tāmaki Makaurau/Auckland in New Zealand takes the other spot with a population of just over 1.6 million.

Indigenous rock art is commonly seen in Australia, as it's still practised by indigenous Aboriginal and Torres Strait Islander people to this day. However, the oldest art of this kind can be seen in the Arnhem Land, where the paintings on the rock date back over 60,000 years. The custodians of Arnhem Land include the Yolngu people, the Bininj people and the Maung people.

On the island of Vanuatu, residents take part in a ritual called gol, or nanggol, which involves them tying vines to their ankles and jumping off stick towers to get as close to the ground as they can. It's thought that a good dive will lead to a good harvest, and many believe this is where bungee jumping originated from.

Māori are the tangata whenua, or indigenous inhabitants, of Aotearoa/New Zealand, and arrived from Polynesia around 1,200 years ago. The first Europeans to sight the country didn't do so until 1642, and never actually set foot on land. It wasn't until the late 18th century that the Pākehā (European) settlement began.

The people of French Polynesia have mailboxes, but they collect their mail from a central post office. So why do they have them? They're used to deliver bread from local bakeries instead of letters!

New Zealand is home to the steepest residential street in the world, which has a slope of 38 degrees – just less than half of a right angle! It's called Baldwin Street and it's in the town of Ōtepoti/Dunedin, if you ever want to tackle the crazy climb!

Sydney Opera House is a landmark that opened in Sydney Harbour, Australia in 1973. The architect was a big fan of sailing, so he added the iconic white domes to the roof to make it look like boat sails were flying in the harbour.

French Polynesia is an archipelago – or a chain of islands – consisting of 121 different land masses spread across the ocean. The most famous islands are Tahiti and Bora Bora, which are just two of the 75 islands that have people living on them.

There are three official languages in New Zealand. English and te reo Māori, are the only spoken ones though, as sign language is the third official language of the country.

New Zealand is a small country, with just over 5 million people living across the North and South Islands, and on its smaller surrounding islands. It's not surprising that this green country has lots of sheep, so many in fact that they outnumber humans 10-to-1!

The geographic North and South Poles are our planet's northernmost and southernmost spots. The North Pole is in the Arctic and the South Pole is in the Antarctic. To reach these areas by land, people must travel over vast and dangerous stretches of ice and snow. An expedition first reached the North Pole in either 1908 or 1909 (the date is disputed). The South Pole was reached in 1911.

Antarctica attracts many scientific explorers as there are 70 permanent research stations on the continent. Scientists visit these stations to study ice and snow, the effects of cold temperatures on various things, the movement of Earth's tectonic plates, meteorites and Antarctic wildlife. They also sample deep ice to read its gas content, which helps them measure climate change over time. Cool!

On average, the windiest place on Earth is Commonwealth Bay in Antarctica. Cold air rolls outward from the South Pole constantly, often reaching speeds over 240 km/h. The daily average is around 80 km/h.

The coldest temperature ever recorded in the Northern Hemisphere was −69.6°C in 1991 in a northern part of Russia. The average winter temperature in the Arctic Circle area is never in the positives, averaging between −6 and −12 °C.

Few people live north of the Arctic Circle, but one group of people has lived in Arctic regions for thousands of years: the Sami. They live in parts of Norway, Sweden, Finland and Russia and traditionally make a living by fishing, or herding reindeer.

Because of its position at the top of the Earth, during the summer months, the Sun doesn't set at all, which earned it the nickname 'the land of the midnight sun'. However, the reverse is true in winter, when there are months at a time of darkness and twilight.

Antarctica has the biggest ice sheet in the world, and it covers 98 percent of the continent! Over 90 percent of the world's ice can be found in Antarctica too and scientists believe if climate change continues and all the ice there melts, the sea level will rise by about 60 metres.

The North Pole and much of the Arctic Circle are not considered a continent because there is no land beneath the ice, unlike in Antarctica. Instead, the whole area is covered in floating ice that measures up to 3 metres thick.

There are actually four different North Poles! There's the point at the northernmost part of the globe, and another that lies under the water. The final two are the magnetic and geomagnetic North Poles, which affect the way magnetism works in the world.

Nobody lives at the North Pole, so no one has ever needed to give it a time zone. As it lies at the top of the world and the lengths of days and nights don't make much sense compared to the rest of the world, visitors just go by whatever time zone they need to!

In 1937, the Soviet Union airdropped four scientists on ice floating at the North Pole so they could set up a temporary research station. When they went back to get them almost a year later, they had floated over 1,600 kilometres away to the Greenland Sea.

As if running a marathon isn't hard enough already, you can also take part in one at the North Pole, where temperatures can reach –29°C. The North Pole Marathon is held every year around a 4.22-kilometre loop through snow and ice.

# FUN

Some facts don't fit so neatly into tidy categories, but we'll let you in on a little secret – they're usually the most fun ones! These pages are filled with the funniest, most unbelievable, most incredible facts that will make you think, wonder, laugh and, most importantly, bring a smile to your face. What are you waiting for?

Buzz Aldrin was the second man on the moon, but he was destined to be there. Before she married his father, Buzz's mother was named Marion Moon! Guess who Buzz Lightyear from *Toy Story* is named after! That's right – Mr Aldrin himself.

Nobody knows for certain who invented the fire hydrants that firefighters use in the United States, because the patent for the invention was torched in a fire in 1836. It's believed that the person who owned the patent was a waterworks engineer called Frederick Graff Sr.

The numbers we use today are called Arabic numerals and they were invented in India around the 6th century! They were introduced to Europe by Indian mathematicians to replace the previous systems, which were largely Roman numerals.

The word muscle comes from the Latin word musculus, which means 'little mouse', because the Romans thought muscles looked like a small rodent crawling around under your skin!

There are over 100 elements in the periodic table, ranging from Actinium to Zirconium, but one letter is missing. Not a single name of a periodic element contains the letter J!

You might have heard of a pride of lions, but what does the 'pride' bit mean? It's called a collective noun and most animals have a special term that refers to a group of them together. You might see a murder of crows sitting on a nearby branch, or a skulk of foxes wandering around. Murder and skulk are the collective nouns.

Leonardo da Vinci, the renowned inventor from the Renaissance period, may have been dyslexic and had trouble reading and writing. He also used 'mirror writing' – he wrote from the right-hand side of a page to the left in his notes!

In 1972, the ground was being excavated for a new building in York, England, when archaeologists discovered a fossilised poo – known as a coprolite – in the ground! It dated back to around AD 800, possibly belonged to a Viking and showed evidence of a meat and bread diet!

During World War II, a Great Dane called Juliana put out an explosive device by weeing on it! She was awarded the Blue Cross medal for bravery, all because she needed to go to the loo!

Painkillers weren't used by dentists until 1772. Rather than having an anaesthetic to have a tooth removed or a filling, you would have people holding you down through the pain! It was only when nitrous oxide was discovered to be a pain reliever that trips to the dentist became bearable.

India has some local adjustments for the four seasons. Winter is from December to February, summer is from March to May, monsoon or rainy season is from June to September and post-monsoon period is October and November.

During the Cold War in the 1960s, the CIA had a program called Acoustic Kitty, which used cats as spies! The cats had microphones surgically inserted into them before they were sent away to listen in on the Russians!

The world's first speeding ticket was given to a man from Kent in England for driving at 8 miles per hour! It was on a road with a speed limit of just 2 miles per hour and the offender was chased for 5 miles by a policeman on a bicycle!

Charles Darwin, who came up with the theory of evolution, was partially inspired by a pirate captain called William Dampier, who made notes and sketched drawings of the unusual plants and animals he saw on his swashbuckling adventures.

The French Government gives good parents a medal! The Médaille de l'Enfance et des Familles, or the Child and Family Medal, was started in the 1920s to encourage adults to have more children, as well as take care of them better.

A French writer called Guy de Maupassant apparently hated the Eiffel Tower so much that he went and ate his lunch under it every day. It was the only place that he could sit and eat in Paris without having to look at the tower!

As only one of the Seven Wonders of the Ancient World – the Great Pyramid of Giza – is still standing, the New Seven Wonders of the World were chosen in the millennium year, 2000. The sites include the rocky ancient city of Petra in Jordan, Rome's Colosseum and India's magnificent Taj Mahal temple.

Valentine's Day was celebrated even in the early 19th century and involved swapping romantic cards and gifts. However, in England, some also sent a 'vinegar valentine', which had ugly cartoons and mean words for the receiver.

There's a bank in Italy called Credem, which will accept cheese in exchange for a money loan! They keep the cheese in a special vault, which is thought to house up to $200 million worth of cheese.

Before gargoyles were added to buildings purely as decoration, they served a function. When it rained, the water would run down the roof and through the gargoyle's mouth, stopping it from rolling down walls and causing damage.

Half of our week is named after Norse gods! Tuesday is named after Tiw, the Norse god of war, while Wednesday is named after Odin, who was sometimes called Woden. The last two gods to be honoured in our days are Thor and Frigg, who gave their names to Thursday and Friday.

The world's biggest search engine, Google, was originally called Backrub. They decided instead to name it after a googol – a huge number beginning with 1, followed by one hundred zeroes!

During World War II, the Catherine Palace in Russia was invaded and a room was stolen. It was called the Amber Room as it had walls covered in amber, but it was taken apart and hasn't been seen since!

The term piggy bank, for a pot where you put spare change – often shaped like a pig – comes from Medieval England. Pygg was a type of clay used to make pots and people often would throw coins into pygg jars. Eventually it was confused with the animal and now we have piggy banks!

If a gargoyle has a body, it isn't a gargoyle, but a grotesque. Gargoyles are normally just heads that have a water spout, but grotesques are full-body figures that are mostly for decoration and never have a spout through the mouth.

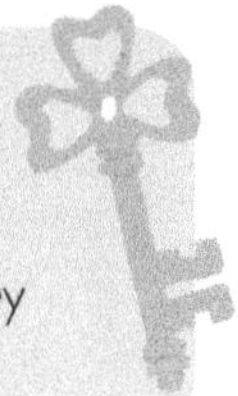

Some people are honoured by 'being given the key to a city', which is a ceremony that dates back to Medieval times. The gates to highly protected cities of the Middle Ages would be locked up at night, but one person would be given the key so they could leave and enter as they wished.

The most popular boy's name in the world is Muhammad (including alternative spellings like Mohammed). It's estimated that over 150 million people across the world have this name – that's over one in one hundred people!

Despite record-breaking temperatures, we're still actually in an ice age! It's the fifth one that Earth has had and we're currently in the interglacial period, which is when the world warms up, melting some of the ice that was around in the time of the woolly mammoth.

There's a statue in Prague of two men weeing while standing in a small pool, but it has a strange secret. Their wee is spelling out quotes from famous books – you can text a message to a special number and they'll start weeing out the words you've sent to them!

In 2008, a group of people in Iran tried to break the record for the world's biggest sandwich, which was packed with ostrich meat. They would've claimed the record; however, a couple of people began to eat the sandwich before it could be measured!

Switzerland is a famously neutral country and refuses to participate in most conflicts, so it was very surprising when they invaded Liechtenstein! 170 of their soldiers got lost on a training exercise and accidentally marched over a kilometre into the tiny European country.

Many of the months of the year are named after gods and goddesses. Janus, the Roman god of beginnings, lends his name to January, May is named after Maia, the Greek goddess of the earth and June is derived from Juno, the Greek goddess queen.

Most countries have a national animal to represent their nation, but Scotland chose a mythical beast – the unicorn! It's been on their coat of arms since the 12th century and they even celebrate National Unicorn Day in Scotland on the 9 April.

When the world's biggest diamond was mined in South Africa, it needed to be sent to England. The Cullinan diamond was sent by steamboat under heavy guard, although that was just a decoy, as the real one was sent in a plain box via post!

Bluetooth, the method of connecting devices wirelessly, is named after a Danish king called Harald Gormsson, who had a rotten tooth that looked, unsurprisingly, blue! He was well-known in Scandinavia for uniting warring tribes around the 10th century.

It's illegal to own just one guinea pig – or other 'social pets' – in Switzerland, because they're happier when they have a friend. You also have to take a course on dog care before you can bring a puppy home too.

Have you ever wondered what the Ms stand for in M&Ms? The initials are the names of the sweets' inventors – Forrest Mars and Bruce Murrie. Forrest had already created the Snickers bar, as well as Maltesers and was the owner of the whole Mars sweet empire.

The longest distance you can walk across the world without needing another form of transport is 22,500 kilometres! You'd need to start in a town called Magadan in Russia, walk through the Middle East, then all the way down to Cape Town in South Africa.

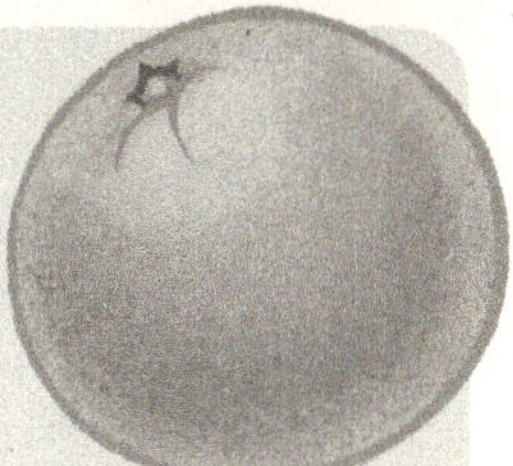

There was no word for the colour orange in the English language until the fruit was imported to the country in the 15th century. Before then, the shade was known as either yellow-red or yellow-saffron!

The human is the only animal in the world that has a chin! Chimps and other closely related species have jaws that slope backwards and even extinct humanoids like Neanderthals didn't have chins, but scientists can't work out why we evolved them!

There are over 200 languages that have been invented just for books, films and television. These include Klingon in *Star Trek*, Elvish in *Lord of the Rings* and Dothraki in *Game of Thrones*.

Did you know animals speak different languages in different countries too? Well not really, but the way different countries describe their sounds changes. For instance, cats meow in English, but in Estonia they go 'nau', while Albania pigs say 'hunk-hunk' instead of oink!

There are seven different types of twin. The most common are identical and fraternal – twins born at the same time but not identical – but the most interesting is the mirror image twin, which is where twins have opposite traits. If one is born left-handed, the other will be right-handed, for example!

A scientist created a computer program to analyse all of recorded history to find out what the most boring day since 1900 was. The answer? 11 April 1954, when absolutely no significant events occurred in the world!

Spoken languages have difficult phrases called tongue-twisters, such as 'she sells sea shells by the sea shore', but there's something similar in sign languages, known as finger-fumblers.

Before you can drive a black cab around London, you need to take a test known as 'the knowledge', which has been around since the middle of the 19th century. Students need to know every street – 25,000 of them – and landmark – 100,000 – within 6 kilometres of Charing Cross in the centre of the city.

If you add up the numbers on opposite sides of any six-sided dice, they will always add up to seven. Six is on the opposite face to one, four and three are always separated by the other numbers, and two and five are the final pair.

Artist Anish Kapoor struck a deal with the creators of Vantablack – a material known as 'the blackest black' – that allowed only him to use it in his art. Another artist, Stuart Semple, developed a pigment he called 'the pinkest pink' and will sell it to anyone in the world, except Anish Kapoor!

A palindrome is a word or phrase that reads the same forwards as it does backwards, like 'racecar' and 'rotator'. 'Weird Al' Yankovic, a musical comedian, once wrote a whole song called 'Bob' in palindromes, including lyrics like 'Won't lovers revolt now?'.

The famous home store IKEA is an acronym, which is why it's always in capitals. It stands for Ingvar Kamprad Elmtaryd Agunnaryd, which is the name of the company's owner. More IKEA catalogues are printed every year than any other book too.

What's the difference between the acronyms BBC and NASA? Well, only one of them is an acronym! NASA is an acronym, because you say it as a single word rather than individual letters, even though it is made up of initials for the North American Space Agency. BBC is an initialism, because you say the individual letters.

The cartoonist Mort Walker coined new terms for lots of the things we see in comics. One of them is grawlix, which are the nonsense symbols like !@#? used when a character says something naughty or that the reader isn't meant to understand.

As of 2024, the tallest living man is from Turkey and is 2.51 metres tall. However, Sultan Kösen would be dwarfed by the tallest man ever. Robert Wadlow was 2.72 metres when he died in 1940.

The famous scientist Stephen Hawking once threw a party for time travellers ... but nobody showed up! He only published the time, date and place for the event after it had passed, so only people who could travel back in time would receive the invitation.

The filling of a Kit Kat bar is made from... Kit Kats! It's strange but the damaged chocolate bars are sent back down the production line, mashed up and used to fill between the wafers and chocolate.

The shape of a Pringle has a name – it's called a hyperbolic paraboloid! The crisp was created in this shape because it meant they could be stacked more securely than a regular flat crisp.

In 17th-century Japan, the feudal lords would purposely install noisy floorboards. They were known as nightingale floors, and made a sound when they were stepped on so the lords knew if someone was creeping – and creaking – around their home.

When you shake a hand with someone you meet, you're actually doing it to show that you're not carrying a weapon! Historians believe that as most people were right-handed and would hold a sword in their right hand, they'd present an empty right hand as a show of peace.

Microsoft's headquarters in Redmond, Washington, in the United States, has the quietest room in the world, where the sound measures in negative decibels: –20.35 decibels to be precise. It's so silent that you can hear your heart beating and bones grinding when you move!

There was a laughing epidemic in Tanzania in 1962, which started in one of the country's schools. The laughter spread between villages and eventually made 14 schools close down while the phenomenon passed! Be careful the next time you tell a joke...